Learning from Behavior

LEARNING FROM BEHAVIOR

How to Understand and
Help "Challenging" Children in School

James E. Levine

Foreword by Sophie Freud

Child Psychology and Mental Health
Hiram E. Fitzgerald and Susanne Ayres Denham, Series Editors

Westport, Connecticut
London

Library of Congress Cataloging-in-Publication Data

Levine, James E.
  Learning from behavior : how to understand and help "challenging"
children in school / by James E. Levine ; foreword by Sophie Freud.
    p. cm. — (Child psychology and mental health, ISSN 1538-8883)
  Includes bibliographical references and index.
  ISBN-13: 978–0–275–99040–4 (alk. paper)
  ISBN-10: 0–275–99040–0 (alk. paper)
 1. Children with disabilities—Education—United States. 2. Behavior
modification—United States. 3. Classroom management—United States.
I. Title.
  LC4031.L455 2007
  370.15'28—dc22   2007009384

British Library Cataloguing in Publication Data is available.

Library of Congress Catalog Card Number: 2007009384

ISBN-13: 978–0–275–99040–4
ISBN-10: 0–275–99040–0
ISSN: 1538–8883

First published in 2007

Praeger Publishers, 88 Post Road West, Westport, CT 06881
An imprint of Greenwood Publishing Group, Inc.
www.praeger.com

Printed in the United States of America

The paper used in this book complies with the
Permanent Paper Standard issued by the National
Information Standards Organization (Z39.48–1984).

10 9 8 7 6 5 4 3 2 1

A practitioner's stance toward inquiry is his attitude toward the reality with which he deals. . . . Through his transaction with the situation, he shapes it and makes himself a part of it. Hence, the sense he makes of the situation must include his own contribution to it. Yet he recognizes that the situation, having a life of its own distinct from his intentions, may foil his projects and reveal new meanings.

Donald A. Schon, The Reflective Practitioner

CONTENTS

SERIES FOREWORD

The twentieth century closed with a decade devoted to the study of brain structure, function, and development that in parallel with studies of the human genome has revealed the extraordinary plasticity of biobehavioral organization and development. The twenty-first century opens with a decade focusing on behavior, but the linkages between brain and behavior are as dynamic as the linkages between parents and children, and children and their environments.

The Child Psychology and Mental Health series is designed to capture much of this dynamic interplay by advocating for strengthening the science of child development and linking that science to issues related to mental health, child care, parenting, education, and public policy.

The series focuses primarily on individual monographs, each dealing with a subject that advances knowledge related to the interplay between normal developmental processes and life-course circumstances that deviate children away from normative developmental pathways. Occasionally, volumes emphasizing broad topics of interest will appear with authors selected to represent the breadth of research, application, and policy issues. The books are intended to reflect the diverse methodologies and content areas encompassed by an age period ranging from conception to late adolescence. Topics of contemporary interest include studies of socioemotional development, behavioral undercontrol, aggression, attachment disorders, substance abuse, and the diverse contextual settings within which development occurs.

Investigators involved with prospective longitudinal studies, large epidemiologic cross-sectional samples, intensely followed clinical cases or those wishing to report a systematic sequence of connected experiments are invited to submit manuscripts. Investigators from all fields in social and behavioral sciences, neurobiological sciences, medical and clinical sciences and education are invited to submit manuscripts with implications for child and adolescent mental health.

In this volume, James Levine addresses a significant question concerning American education: How can teachers help to craft relationships with students that enable students to gain sufficient control of their behavior to benefit from the educational context? There is a crisis in youth mental health, and schools provide an environment that affords opportunities to help children cope with and resolve developmental challenges. As Levine points out, a key aspect of helping children cope is to provide teachers with the tools necessary to establish trusting relationships, to understand principles of behavioral management, and to organize interventions that address problem behavior from a broad systemic perspective. This is a foundational volume that will both challenge teachers and offer them a tool kit for action.

Hiram E. Fitzgerald
Susanne Ayres Denham
Series Editors

FOREWORD

It is an honor and a joy for me to introduce a book that I encouraged the author to write. I did so because I knew from my long years of teaching social work students and from my own clinical practice of the great need for expert guidance to help children with serious and complex psychological problems that become such a challenge to them, their parents, their schools, the mental health professionals who try to deal with them, and the community in which they must eventually find a dignified place. Sophisticated brain research and many kinds of psychotropic medications have replaced, in most settings, the methods I was trained in so many years ago: longtime and somewhat unfocused play therapy, relentless oedipal interpretations, and the determined blaming of desperate parents who are overwhelmed by their puzzling children. While some may view this shift as a progressive development, it is often not an ideal answer for troubled children, entailing the uncomfortable hazard of premature or excessive medication. Along with a medicinal approach, educators and mental health professionals have also turned to a so-called behavioral approach, with somewhat mechanical positive and negative reward and deprivation systems.

One of the many strengths of *Learning from Behavior* is the author's stance in a middle ground between these various approaches. He is not averse to cautious medicinal interventions or to a meaningful reward system. But all his interventions are based on a solid, trusting relationship between the child and the helping person, a relationship that has curative aspects by its very nature. His goal, as implied in the title, is to understand the meaning each symptom has for the child and to engage the child as a collaborator in his or her own treatment. Each plan is individualized, developed for the specific child in light of his or her strengths and vulnerabilities. I really love the caring, respectful, humanistic basis on which all of Dr. Levine's interventions are based. We get to know these troubled children in the many helpful vignettes included in the text. These are not malevolent children—not even those with a diagnosis of oppositional disorder—out to combat the adult world. Dr. Levine's children are anxious, confused, depressed, traumatized, and desperate to preserve their battered self-esteem and shreds of dignity. They have angry meltdowns when the requirements of their environments overwhelm their fragile identities.

I wish a book such as this had been available when I taught students social work practice. While the book is aimed at teachers and school mental health professionals, many helping professionals find themselves in unexpected situations in which understanding and helping children become of the essence. As an instructor of social work students who mostly hoped to become clinicians, I was always looking for a succinct primer-type book that would deftly integrate theory and practice and prepare all my students for such interventions, regardless of their specialty. Now, finally, we have precisely such a book. It surely should become a basic reader in the education of any mental health professional who may at some point be faced with diagnosis and/or treatment and/or consultation to a setting that includes troubled children.

Oh, how I wish I had had the 26 commandments of chapter 3, or the 10 principles of behavioral planning of chapter 4, at my fingertips when I was a young family worker in a Boston tenement district—or, for that matter, when I raised my own children. Indeed, while the book is meant for helping professionals, parents will eagerly embrace the principles outlined by Dr. Levine. Do not make behavioral plans with goals that are either reached or failed; a good enough result will last longer than one effort at perfection. Avoid either-or, rigid thinking. Give children credit for effort, and save them from hopeless despair. All the concepts in the book are so clearly explained that any thoughtful parent or caregiver could understand and apply them. This also implies that I consider the author's method of working with children as an approach that could benefit any children in their inevitable crises of growing up and any parents, teachers, or mental health professionals who want to deal with and understand difficult situations as expertly and caringly as possible.

The author was one of my most talented students, whose career has already made a dramatic impact on the lives of many troubled children (and their parents). Such a happy turn of events is the best that can happen to us as teachers. We thank and applaud Dr. Levine for writing this rich yet succinct, wonderfully compassionate book that expands on his knowledge and wisdom, benefiting innumerable families in many different settings.

Sophie Freud, MSW, PhD
Professor Emerita of the Simmons
College School of Social Work

ACKNOWLEDGMENTS

I am the fortunate product of many fine thinkers over the years. More specifically, Sophie Freud, PhD, offered kindness, guidance, and mentorship both during my doctoral studies at Simmons College and in this effort, and I remain deeply gratified by her knowledge and skill. Miles Morrissey, LICSW, and Roger Anderson, LICSW, provided much-appreciated support, friendship, and feedback. My colleague Rebecca Ettelson, PhD, added thoughtful editorial ideas. Debbie Carvalko, my editor at Praeger, supplied the gentle encouragement and clear thinking to help this project across the finish line. And to my wife, Cheryl Campbell, and children, Jeremy and Maya, I can say that my appreciation is surpassed only by my awe for your caring, thoughtfulness, and love. This book signifies the efforts of us all, even if the end product reflects my own tone and style.

I am grateful as well to the countless teachers, school counselors, principals, families, and, of course, the many children who have allowed me into the day-to-day workings of their lives. Perhaps it sounds like a cliché, but I have genuinely received as much as I have given. Truly, it has been a privilege.

A NOTE ABOUT GENDER USE

The word *he* is used rather than the more cumbersome construction *he or she* or, for that matter, the word *she*. The rationale is that, simply put, substantially more boys than girls are placed on behavioral plans, though there is apparently no formal research to support such a statement. But visit any school and speak with counselors or special education teachers, and it is clear that it is a male-dominated intervention. Thus the word *he* has been chosen here. It is not intended to suggest that girls do not have struggles in school or require helping interventions of all kinds, and I hope no offense is taken by such a choice.

LAYOUT OF THE BOOK

The first chapter of the book addresses the notions of listening and learning so as to *understand* behavior. In doing so, it provides a theoretical backdrop for the amalgam of practical clinical interventions described in chapter 3. The second chapter describes a set of mental health diagnoses and the characteristics associated with children who manifest severe behavioral challenges. Chapter 4 amplifies the values intrinsic to setting up formal behavioral interventions and offers both theoretical and clinical rationales for creating a model consistent with them. The subsequent chapter describes a specific school-based model that incorporates and reflects these ideas in practice. Chapter 6 demonstrates the application of this model to particular case studies, utilizing as well the various strategies described earlier in the book. The concluding chapter presents an array of ideas and recommendations for going forward. Clearly much thinking, research, and commitment toward enhancing both our conceptual understanding and our practice methods continues to be needed.

This book is based on an accumulation of many years of clinical practice, observation, thinking, and discourse. It is intended to add to the ongoing dialogue about what will help children amid the combined challenges of developmental, family, and cultural change. The hope is that at its core, this book will add another voice that augments our repertoire of *best practices* and, at the same time, offers a new way to frame the discussion on children's needs, one that is based on the recognized importance of meaningful relationships and an enhanced understanding of childhood behavior. It is intended for a wide range of clinical practitioners, especially those who work in school settings as well as guidance staff, special educators, regular education teachers, alternative classroom staff, school administrators, graduate students in the mental health disciplines, and, notably, parents who are invested in reflecting on the kinds of behavioral and preventive strategies that can thoughtfully be employed in the service of children's needs.

INTRODUCTION

What is our understanding of the child's behavior? A simple question lies at the heart of this book. It is a mantra that reveals itself in approaches to assessment, intervention, follow-up, and the many strategies offered here to help children. This apparent simplicity, however, is deceptive, as our understanding can be obscured or diverted by layers of competing behaviors, words, ways of presenting oneself, and so on. The question is easier to pose than to answer.

Alex is 11 and constantly in trouble during the school day. His teacher, experienced in the ways of sixth graders, sees him as willful and stubborn. Alex refuses to do things that are asked of him, jokes with other students during lectures, and has a sarcastic edge to his comments. The common perception of Alex is that he is spoiled and uncooperative, probably to the level of having oppositional defiant disorder. Confrontations with him over his behavior, and the requisite trips to the principal, have done nothing to alter this pattern. The removal of privileges, at home as well as in school, leads to even more challenging behavior. The cause of all this misbehavior? Recently, it was discovered during a clinical evaluation that Alex has both anxiety and severe depression. He describes the anxiety as "wearing him out," and the combination of these two disorders leaves him angry, dejected, and unable to process new information clearly. As this vignette indicates, the misbehavior may be clear in the eyes of the beholders, but understanding its cause and thus its solution takes more; it takes a kind of learning from and about behavior. That learning, based on careful listening and the questioning that precedes it, is an art. It is a basic art that all who care about and work with children—from teachers to counselors and parents—can and should develop.

The word *behavior* conjures up many different meanings and implications, few of them positive. When the word is used, especially in the context of discussing children, an obvious assumption is at hand: there is a problem to be conquered. We talk about decreasing, dealing with, and various forms of managing behavior. Yet so often we do not understand the meaning of the behavior for that individual or what it represents. Is it attention seeking, task-avoidant, or a manifestation of a medical problem? Does it signify a sensory regulation or communication issue? Is this a child who is pleading for consistent and clear limits? Are there adults—or even just one—who provide the kind of relationship children need to simultaneously take intelligent risks and hold on to a sense of calm? Each of these areas suggests a different approach to intervention, so the idea of management must equally be based on a more specific and nuanced understanding. One question I always ask when consulting on a case is, Has anyone asked the child what the behavior means? This query often elicits a surprised response from parents and school staff. If the child has no insights to offer, is there a sense that he wants (or is willing to accept) help in understanding it? The approach offered in this book is based on the perspective that children, especially those having behavioral difficulties, often require assistance in making coherent sense of their actions and that any rewards included in the intervention process are a vehicle for learning rather than the sole reason for change. The specific behavioral model described in this book therefore is derived from this belief in an inherently educational, skill-based approach to teaching children about behavior. Such an approach ultimately sets a foundation for children to develop greater mastery of their behavior.

Understanding children's behavior, it seems to me, is at the root of effective helping by adults. If this sounds like an obvious statement, observe the ways in which many behavioral plans are used in schools. In contrast to the idea that there should first be some kind of working theory about what might be driving a child's challenging behavior, there is often a cursory assessment of the child, and then some sort of strategic intervention is sprung. Even the creation and increasing use of functional behavioral assessments (FBA, discussed later) have not altered the typical array of interventions used in schools, such as removal from class and other negative consequences. Most FBAs, in fact, seem to be grounded mainly in legal requirements concerning a child's placement and questions about staffing ratios and specialized services. How is it possible to teach children about their behavior if we have not taken the time to solidify our understanding of its meaning and context?

Furthermore, it is the personal act of *trying* to understand, in a relational context, that often leads to improvement, whether this takes the form of active listening or a quiet walk together around the block. One rarely hears about behavior plans in the same sentence as client-centered therapeutic approaches, but I think it useful to look at the potential overlap. Older models, such as Carl Rogers's client-centered therapy, and newer ones, such as motivational interviewing, have components that might be incorporated. Both these approaches, developed in part to deepen people's engagement in the process of psychotherapy, aim to empower clients, rather than emphasize the authority of the therapist; that is, they are centered around client concerns and their notion of change, rather than around the therapist's agenda. When utilized as intended, they entail thoughtful listening and a genuine concern for clients' stories. While these models were first created with an adult population in mind, the ideas are relevant in considering how to help children as well. For example, Miller and Rollnick (2002) refer to the idea of change talk,[1] which includes the processes of elaborating, reflecting, summarizing, and affirming. As this book shows, these same types of processes should be inherent in the feedback given to children who are helped by behavioral interventions. In simple terms, children's relationships matter, whether during psychotherapy or their minute-to-minute interactions with adults in school. It should not be an either-or process; children need consequences for their behavioral choices at the same time that they need adults who are willing to listen and connect with them around learning about the ins and outs of their behavior.

The purpose of this book, then, is to advance the proposed connection between understanding behavior and developing creative interventions for changing it. Each strategy is reliant on this main idea. To help children in a genuine way, we need to continue to search for ways to understand their experience and establish interventions that resonate with their developmental, social, psychological, and behavioral needs. Moreover, the behavioral approach described in chapter 5 offers a specified format for intervention, but how it is implemented is based on children's disparate needs and skills. Little previous literature has been devoted to such a notion, that behavioral interventions can offer both a specific method and language and, at the same time, be flexible and sensitive to developmental and experiential differences in how they are applied.

There is an important caveat in the development of any behavioral plan that is of particular relevance for work with children, and it underlies all the principles advanced in this book. Behaviors may represent what a child cannot communicate verbally. Given the importance of this concept, it will be repeated here: behaviors may reflect what a child is unable to convey verbally. So we need to question and to listen, to help the child verbalize where possible and, at the least, help him to vent what he cannot communicate in other acceptable ways. When a child acts out due to an inability to communicate, this inability can be due to issues of language, cognitive development, or traumatic experience. All of us—including the child—need to learn from these behaviors to help in the creation of more successful ones.

For example, Sarah, a 12-year-old girl with both a speech delay and undiagnosed depression, had been placed on a behavioral intervention at school based on the goal of reducing the behaviors interconnected with her depression—intermittent rudeness and tearful, angry outbursts that included swearing and yelling at teachers and peers. These behaviors were perceived as purposefully oppositional—that is, based on her supposed wish to upset others and hold a one-up position on them—rather than as a manifestation of her unhappiness, a scenario magnified by the school's surprise and unease over the fact that she was "a girl acting in such a way." When I observed and then spoke with her, she seemed to feel badly about these behaviors when they emerged and even worse about her speech delay. In many ways she acted out what she lacked the opportunity—and capacity—to articulate. Sarah reported that people in school had "pulled away" from her, leaving her feeling isolated and with no one to talk with. The behavioral intervention in place exacerbated her behavior since there was no built-in space for her to make sense of the behavior; the plan merely reacted to her actions and, to her way of thinking, simply offered further confirming evidence of her inability to get along in the world. It was not until we changed the behavioral approach to an intervention based on the concept of *preventing* problems and allowed her regular feedback time to process and discuss events (this will be more fully described later in the book) that her behavior began, tentatively, to change. The behavioral intervention required more of a relational aspect to it, an adult willing to sit with her for a short time, rather than mere written notations letting her know that she had once again blown it with her actions. Furthermore, the school convinced her parents to bring her to outpatient therapy. This was not a miracle approach. It was simply an attempt to establish a better understanding of Sarah's presentation, enable her to give voice to her own experience, and, in a supportive environment, offer her alternate ways to communicate this.

Another example: Tim, a nine-year-old described as a boy who "tries hard" and is eager to please, was referred for consultation due to periodic and unexplained rages in school. These rages took the form of screaming fits, pounding on his desk with his fists, and, on one particularly difficult day, ramming his head against a locker. Consequences, trips to the principal, notes home to his parents—none of this had impacted his behavior. A behavioral intervention that relied on numbers of points for misbehavior and that was often used by this particular school district was set in motion. In this approach the school chose particular goals and told Tim what he needed to do and what negative consequences would occur if he was unsuccessful. Tim's behavior worsened. The school switched to a different type of intervention, one in which the school continued to select behavioral goals but Tim would now earn specified rewards if he was cooperative. While the number of incidents decreased, the level of rage when he did explode was frightening. My role, coming in after all of this had transpired, was initially to suggest that the current plan be stopped until there was a better theory as to what was underlying this behavior. In my mind, trauma needed to be ruled in or out. Given his relatively recent history of explosiveness, lack of relevant neurological or developmental history, and silence over what was happening (in spite of being an articulate child), it seemed fairly likely that events in his life were reflected in this behavior. The short story is that there was serious domestic violence at home, which Tim felt powerless to stop, and amid the chaos and violence, he had developed posttraumatic stress disorder (PTSD). (PTSD is discussed in chapter 2, but in brief, it entails a powerful physiological and emotional response to certain external events and internal states.) In this instance a behavioral intervention had motivated him to cease his own angry behavior, but it had the effect of shutting him down for only so long until he could not contain himself any longer. As such, the intervention squelched his only way of letting people around him know that something was seriously wrong. I am not suggesting that the behavior was adaptive or helpful, but it did serve as a form of communication. Notification to the Department of Social Services and other extrinsic interventions, such as family counseling and anger management training for the father, reduced the chaos in his daily life, and the later use of a behavioral intervention was needed only for a short time once there was increased safety and calm at home.

These examples illustrate that whatever the basis, it is critical that adults aim to understand the meaning of the targeted behaviors from the child's perspective before implementing a behavioral intervention. Attempts to eliminate behaviors that represent an important, nonverbal form of communication may contribute to a poor outcome as these are likely to result in a depressed, frustrated, and resentful child. Children are not simply younger versions of adults: they often employ a different way of communicating their needs that does not match the predominantly verbal and rational manner of adults. Viewing behavior as a form of communication is a prerequisite to this endeavor to fully understand the child's behavior.

Thus an emphasis on understanding children's behaviors as embedded in a broader biopsychosocial context (Saari, 1992, writes clearly about the biopsychosocial perspective,[2] although a host of writers have commented on this topic) must remain an integral consideration of case assessments and is a necessary precursor to implementing formal behavioral plans. The biopsychosocial approach, in short, takes into account the broad factors that affect an individual's life, including one's biological traits, level and quality of social supports, and psychological health. It refutes the narrow stance that some branches of the mental health field have at times adopted in making psychiatric diagnoses. This perspective, then, is consistent with the larger mission of good mental health practice. If we are truly to adopt such a perspective, we must maintain our awareness of the larger system as well as the individual child, even when mandated to focus on the child's specific presentation of behavior.

Finally, another caveat to keep in mind is that no approach is always successful. That includes the behavioral model and the various strategies described in this book. In spite of the surprisingly prevalent notion that childhood is a simple time, children are complex, and it can be a difficult and time-consuming challenge to make sense of their behavior and generate interventions that work. Sometimes we struggle with how to help a particular child, and at other times, we know what to do but lack the opening to intervene. When there are numerous children in a classroom or school that require in-depth problem solving, a lack of available time or resources may hinder our capacity to help. Teachers frequently allude to these limitations, especially when they have four or five (or even more) children in their classrooms with complicated behavioral, developmental, and learning presentations. In addition, we often sense that we are powerless to alter the conditions affecting children outside of school.

In spite of such challenges, we need to do our best to address the lives of these children. The goal of this book, then, is to offer specific approaches to providing help as well as a way of conceptualizing how to do so. Even—as noted earlier—the behavioral model depicted here must be used flexibly and in a manner consistent with our understanding of each child, as should the different strategies discussed throughout. These are key points. There is no pretense that they solve children's problems. However, they serve to advance our knowledge base and our repertoire of helping strategies. In that sense this book is a step forward, not an end point.

My own interest in this work was stimulated by, among other things, a stint as a music therapy intern in England during the late 1970s. My mentor, the program director and probably the most energetic and committed person I have ever met, was a determined woman named Lindy Wyman who believed that any of the proverbial brick walls blocking her way were there solely to be knocked down. This she did with sheer kindness and good-heartedness. The clinic, located in a drastically poor section of London, was established to serve refugees from Bangladesh who fled their country to escape the violence stemming from the war of 1971. It was at that time that Pakistan and Bangladesh separated into distinct countries, based on Bangladesh's drive for independence, but the distress resulting both from the activities of war and the subsequent relocation to a strange country left a great many people stunned, angry, and grieving. My work, usually with children and adolescents, taught me a whole new meaning of trauma. The children, principally the older ones, seethed with fury as they strove to adapt to a changed world with shifting expectations. In spite of the fact that some of them had lived in England for five years or more, it was as though they were frozen at an earlier time. Later research into the manifestations of trauma revealed that this is not an unusual phenomenon, but it was a shock to witness directly amid such intensity and poverty.

I observed some of the different approaches used to try to help these children. It was evident to me, even a young mental health worker, that behavioral plans trailed the other interventions as a primary source of help. It was the relational bonds that mattered, the safety and security that could be mustered in the hopes of helping these children—and their parents—settle into an unfamiliar world. What we now commonly refer to as cultural competence was clearly an important factor as well. One had to make an honest attempt to try to grasp something about Bangladeshi history and traditions to build a foundation for connecting with these families. The children were especially attuned to figuring out when their culture was misunderstood or, worse, discounted by the more dominant groups.

It appeared that the different forms of behavioral intervention only succeeded when at least some degree of social connection was first established. This pattern was repeated for me in the various work settings that followed, including a group home for male juvenile offenders and a locked ward for children with autistic disorders, along with what was then commonly referred to as childhood schizophrenia. This was followed by stints as a program manager for children in specialized foster care, a clinic-based therapist, and then a consultant to schools. What I observed was that behavioral interventions were regularly put to use and assumed to be helpful, but with little training for staff, limited attention to the features that underlie their actual effectiveness, and a crippling lack of connection to the other factors that shape children's lives. While there is much known about using consequences to shape and alter behavior, there seems to me even more that we have not yet synthesized as to how to put this knowledge into practice. Therein lies the purpose for writing this book.

Learning from Behavior

Chapter 1

STOP, LOOK, AND LISTEN: UNDERSTANDING BEHAVIOR AND THE SIGNIFICANCE OF RELATIONSHIPS

It is this very question—why do we need to understand the meaning of a child's behavior—that should inspire ways for us to seek and develop effective methods for working with children. Because challenging behavior, especially in the classroom, can cause any of us to feel that things are about to spiral out of control, a common—and understandable— response by adults is simply to want to put an immediate end to the behavior. Often, we experience the child as acting in a purposeful, even assaultive way. Yet the same presentation of behavior can stem from very different situations.

For example, Tom, an 11-year-old boy referred by his school for non-compliance and poor academic performance, was assumed to have attention-deficit/hyperactivity disorder (ADHD) based on the constellation of symptoms he presented. Yet, with further assessment of his school records (his parents did not respond to the school's request to come in), it was discovered that his developmental history indicated the likelihood of severe physical trauma as a different or additional diagnosis. His symptoms included inattention and lack of persistence, impulsivity, high motor activity, poor time management, and disinhibited behavior. However, posttraumatic stress disorder (PTSD) and lead paint poisoning can evoke an identical presentation to that of ADHD.

In addition, Tom had a consistent need to control the people and events surrounding him, rageful reactions when things did not go his way, and a kind of wary style that continually left him on edge. All these characteristics are associated with trauma. This implies that it is only through careful assessment of a whole range of relevant factors that we can begin to make sense of a child's behavior. In Tom's case, a referral to special education to help with academics (his performance began to decline when the work was no longer based on rote learning and factual recall) and a connection with a therapist sensitive to and experienced with issues of trauma contributed to significant improvement in his academic and behavioral functioning over the next six months. No formal intervention for ADHD was needed, though Tom did require additional assistance in developing organizational skills. Notably, he also relied on the support of a school team perceptive of his many needs and willing to respond kindly to his anxious hypervigilance. For example, teachers often allowed Tom to make his own choices, such as when to leave the classroom, based on their perception of him as someone who needed to feel that he was in control. They also reminded him gently when he needed to get back on task. Fortunately for Tom, this team chose not to treat him as a child with purposeful acting-out issues.

Another example, one that further illustrates the importance of understanding the meaning and purpose of behavior, is of Clarence, a 10-year-old fourth grader, who was reported by his parents and teacher to tell "tall tales" on a regular basis. No one could establish a clear sense of this behavior because it occurred on an inconsistent basis without any obvious purpose. The family's use of escalating negative consequences—bigger if he lied about something he did, smaller if he acknowledged the act—made no difference. The family tended to remove privileges, such as video games and television time, and there was a dramatic increase in the amount of time taken away from him if lying was involved. In fact, such consequences seemed to invite more lying and an attitude of "go ahead, take whatever you want." Clearly his parents and teachers were frustrated. To me, it seemed imperative to develop some kind of working theory about the behavior, and mine was that he was depressed and, at least in school, lying to avoid situations in which he might encounter failure. It helped to know that he was a perfectionist and often melted down if he made the smallest error, signifying that his self-worth was consistently threatened. The act of lying can serve different purposes, so the development of an initial hypothesis relied on such teacher and parent reports. The interventions that followed were based on this theory, including the recommendation for an evaluation for depression. In school, he was offered the prospect of reading to kindergarten students, giving him an opportunity to shine in a low-pressure situation. A surprise to many people, Clarence readily accepted this. Teachers also asked him, when it seemed that he was telling a fictitious story, if this was the "truth" or a "wish," which allowed him a way out of the deception. Finally, the adults in his life agreed to avoid confronting him in the moment, asking him to "think about it" and let them know if there was another way to explain a story or act.

In combination, these interventions contributed to a significant decrease in his number of lies. The diagnosis of depression, known more formally in this case as dysthymia, a low-level but regular occurrence of depression, came later and led to both individual therapy and consultation to the family. In this situation, the hypothesis was correct, though that certainly is not always the outcome. The point is that there needs to be some overarching theory about what underlies the child's behavior, with careful interventions that follow logically from an initial set of assumptions. Equally important, we must be willing to challenge and change our assumptions—and therefore shift interventions—when they appear to be wrong.

Children with learning disabilities are notoriously viewed as behavior problems. The perception of them as task-avoidant is sometimes framed as a lack of motivation or caring rather than an understandable—although certainly not constructive—response to their learning challenges. It is not unusual, for example, to find children with reading disabilities who act out whenever they might be called on to read aloud in class. Similarly, children with autistic spectrum disorders are often portrayed in this way. Finding that so many are described in such terms suggests that perhaps something else is going on; that is, it says something about the struggle over coping with specific learning or other disabilities, rather than revealing some kind of moral deficiency in these children. A specific example follows: over the past year, I have consulted on four cases of high school boys diagnosed with Asperger's syndrome who refused to reveal the thinking behind their work, typically in math, but also in story composition. Given the similarities of these adolescents' presentations and the corresponding complaints about them, is it possible that this seeming lack of regard for what is important to educators has more to do with the specifics of Asperger's than with purposeful acting out? The thesis of this book is that such an outcome means schools and other institutional settings—and all the rest of us who spend time with children—need to know more about what underlies the behavior of children.

Many books discuss the issue of behavior management and offer helpful advice on strategies for accomplishing this. Saphier and Gower (1997) suggest that it is essential to "match" interventions to the specific child,[3] a pertinent reminder that should underlie any efforts at implementing behavioral strategies. My concern, however, is that there is sometimes a sense that children are objects to be manipulated according to a set formula; that is, we know that children with ADHD present a subset of particular symptoms and that children with Asperger's syndrome display another, but there is more to be said about behavior than merely the presentation of symptoms. We have to know about the situations and conditions in which such symptoms occur.

This notion of *context,* referred to more academically as the biopsychosocial perspective, honors the rationale for understanding the whole constellation of a person's presentation. More specifically, it accounts for the physiology, temperament, psychological development, and interpersonal and social circumstances of the child, rather than any single area of functioning. Too often, in the current climate, we are pressed to make snap judgments about children's presenting mental health concerns. As other writers have observed, it may be wider aspects of the school environment—is the child being bullied, for example—as opposed to the child's presenting behavior that should be the primary, or at least equivalent, focus of change.

While numerous descriptors indicate what is wrong with children, surprisingly few give us a picture of their success, competence, or mastery. I have countless examples of children who can tell me in stark detail what is deemed bad about them but are stumped when asked to describe the more appealing aspects of how they act. It is as if they have no mental picture for this, not just a lack of words to articulate their thoughts. Mary, 13 years old and streetwise far beyond her years, supplied me with a laundry list of her problematic behaviors that included, in her terms, a bad attitude, disrespect, lying, stealing, and not giving a damn about other people. She simply gaped at me when I asked about any positive traits she might be able to identify—her look represented one of almost total incomprehension. Yet I heard from staff in her school that she was responsible for younger siblings, took care of an alcoholic mother, and showed up at school every day. In addition, she was described as bright, able to link academic material with her experience, and an able writer and storyteller. None of this was identified by Mary during our initial discussion. She was a living example of what some therapists refer to as *problem focused.*

As such, the mental health notion of a *strengths perspective* (Glicken, 2003; Saleebey, 1996),[4,5] along with what is now being referred to as *positive psychology,* may be helpful for children when translated into a clinical action plan. The strengths perspective, according to these authors, is a therapy approach that emphasizes an individual's personal capacities and coping skills. Rather than focusing on what is wrong, there is greater attention to how one has survived similar or other challenges. What competencies did the person bring to bear? How was the child able to mobilize in such a way? Without a strong relationship between the individual and the therapist, the strengths approach can seem like an empty exercise. But when such a relationship is firmly in place, clients often find this emphasis on their skills and aptitudes an energizing and renewing experience. This is fine for children who attend therapy, but a more systemic, global, and accessible approach is ultimately required. Another way of saying this is that schools must attempt to convert children's need for positive regard into active and consistent practice. It only furthers the process when parents are able to do the same at home.

BEHAVIORAL INTERVENTIONS

There are various ways to construct behavioral interventions. Most of these plans are set up to focus on individual behaviors, often referred to as *target behaviors,* with an emphasis on reducing or eliminating them. In behavioral terminology, the process is called *extinction.* At times, behavioral interventions are generated that focus on group behavior, and it is not unusual for classrooms to employ such an approach. These tend to focus on desirable classroom behaviors such as listening, following directions, and being kind toward others. Some teachers reward their students for completed work such as reading a certain number of books. Typically, though, behavioral interventions are instituted for children who are struggling with their behavior.

As noted, there are numerous ways to devise behavioral plans. In fact, most settings implement these interventions in their own individualized—and sometimes idiosyncratic—ways. Areas of difference relate both to the *philosophy* and techniques for implementation; that is, some settings rely on the use of positive reinforcement (the provision of positive rewards, such as tangibles or privileges, now commonly referred to as *positive behavioral supports*); others tend to adopt the use of negative reinforcement (eliminating a negative event by providing, for example, no-homework passes for children who hate to spend time outside of school engaged in anything even resembling academic work); and others emphasize punishment (the removal of privileges or the application of a negative reinforcer, such as detention or dismissal from the classroom). Most systems are fairly consistent in their choice of how to provide consequences for both positive and negative behavior, consistent with how they view children, their experience and training in using behavioral interventions, and their perception of what works. As such, there are basic and fundamental differences in how behavioral interventions are employed. In addition, how children are introduced to and included in these plans differs widely, and this idea will be discussed further on in the book.

Historically, disputes between supporters and opponents of behavioral therapies have revealed powerful differences in relation to clinical thinking, approach, and even worldview. Volumes have been devoted to the general discussion. Disagreements over effectiveness and ethical justification have been vigorously debated among mental health professionals (McNeil, 1996) as well as nonprofessionals.[6] As a prototypical example, Eisenberger and Cameron (1996) contended that, used properly, behavioral interventions could lead to the generalization of personal creativity.[7] Conversely, Kohn (1993) argued that such approaches hinder intrinsic motivation and, ultimately, "rupture" relationships.[8] On the surface, these competing notions appear to be mutually exclusive.

Few attempts have been made to reconcile the use of behavioral interventions with other, psychodynamically oriented approaches (Wachtel, 1977).[9] Wachtel observed that relationally based therapists, including psychoanalysts, tend to view behavior therapies as coercive and subject to the whims of what those in power believe is socially acceptable behavior. He noted that, conversely, behaviorists believe that other forms of therapy ignore or deny the influence of the therapist's values and assumptions; in addition, they contend that current, real-life experiences create the most effective conditions for facilitating change. Wachtel's goal, therefore, was to establish a different perspective for understanding such therapy as well as methods for integrating these divergent ideas. For example, he argued that the removal of symptoms is not the goal of behaviorists but that, instead, this form of therapy is of value because it helps "the person to actively confront the major issues, inhibitions, and distortions in his life" (p. 292). There is, however, little evidence in the subsequent literature for widespread acceptance of Wachtel's ideas or of any attempts to further assimilate these paradigms.

As noted, Kohn is certainly not alone in his mistrust of behavioral interventions. A critical argument against their use is that they can come to be viewed as primary—and sole—solutions to behavior problems rather than as aspects of a larger approach to helping children. Children's individual expressions of behavioral issues represent a broad range of issues, both personal and environmental, and our interventions must reflect this reality. Simply put, this notion mirrors the actual circumstances of children's lives, and intervening only in one area or another does not confront the totality of what they face—and reveal to us. When implemented correctly and within a broader perspective for offering help, behavioral interventions are a fundamental tool for teaching children to understand and change their patterns of behavior. Ideally, these interventions are employed as an adjunct to other supportive approaches; within the classroom, there must be a robust curriculum, proper pacing, clear expectations and rules, and strong teaching. No school-based behavioral intervention will be effective in lieu of these other factors.

Parents and other caregivers, of course, have similar responsibilities and challenges in terms of generating a home environment that is safe, has explicit rules and expectations, and provides support and nurturing. It is no different from a school setting in the sense that the environment needs to be conducive to children displaying positive behavior. Without such structure and supports, a behavior plan may simply be an exercise in futility.

Moreover, Kohn raises the question of whether, via grades and other forms of extrinsic rewards, we rob children of self-determination, which, he believes, leads to reduced motivation. To me, the issue is not the behavioral intervention itself, but rather how it is framed, introduced, and implemented. As this book demonstrates, such interventions must be collaborative, educational, and, above all, respectful; that is, they are reliant on meaningful relationships. Utilized in these ways, a behavioral intervention can enhance self-determination, and thus a child's level of motivation is not necessarily a casualty of such interventions. Kohn's perspective, however, is a critical reminder that behavioral plans should be used cautiously and thoughtfully, rather than as mindless tools we employ simply because they are available and may increase compliance. Consideration of who receives behavioral interventions, and why, needs to be part of the equation.

A corollary to the concerns raised by Kohn is that one must be clear about the specific *target* of the intervention. The idea that a parent—or school—might reinforce children for receiving top grades is conceptually different than rewarding a highly anxious child for participating in class or, for that matter, stepping into the school building. In this book, behavioral interventions are employed more from the perspective of helping children to cope, to learn about their behavior and attempt new approaches for addressing problems, than as a mind-set emphasizing the need for them to be good or motivated in an adult-defined way. For a number of children, a successful behavioral intervention results in their becoming increasingly *available* for learning. It is just as much about the process as the outcome.

My experience is that school professionals are sometimes unaware or deny their use of behavioral interventions. They may refer instead to "incentives" or "natural consequences," but at times, they resort to the exact practices they profess not to employ. Marble jars, check sheets, the promise of a pizza party, or going out for a favorite activity—these are all interventions that reward desired behaviors. Similarly, they may punish children for particular misdeeds, whether this takes the form of denying privileges or sending them off to an authority figure such as a principal. Each of these actions, no matter what it is called, is essentially a form of *operant conditioning*.

This term, usually associated with the groundbreaking work of B. F. Skinner, inspires some teachers, parents, and clinicians and is loathed by others. Operant conditioning was first developed by Thorndike and known initially as *instrumental conditioning*. As opposed to *classical conditioning*, in which involuntary responses are elicited—the famous example is Pavlov's dogs, which were conditioned to salivate every time they heard a bell, even without the presence of food—operant conditioning refers to the principle of behavior-response (or, more formally, behavior-stimulus); that is, operant conditioning relies on the notion that every behavior is shaped by the subsequent response to it. It is this form of conditioning that underlies the belief that behaviors require specific consequences that will either bolster or decrease their occurrence. This, of course, is dependent on the perceived desirability of the behavior. Every ABC chart used by school psychologists rests on this same principle. In addition, what traditionally has been known more broadly as behavior modification is also predicated on operant conditioning (Goldstein, 1995).[10]

As noted, there are numerous critics of this model. A theme of these criticisms is that the model is simplistic and ignores an individual's free will and the influence of one's thoughts, feelings, and choices. Rather than creating an intellectual and practical schism between this model and other forms of helping, however, we should be exploring ways to combine and expand our repertoire of approaches, both theoretically and in action. With the vast number of behavioral interventions in place and the many children who go to therapy, some attempt to integrate what works in each realm would seem a logical next step.

In spite of the insistent voices on both sides, there remains limited information concerning specific ideas for developing, establishing, and evaluating behavioral interventions with disadvantaged populations, especially children. Thyer (1988) contended, for example, that the field of social work has assembled a substantive level of scholarship in what he refers to as behavioral social work.[11] Thyer later acknowledged, however, that this scholarship has not been effectively translated into clinical training and practice. Similarly, Viadero (2002) asserted that research concerning student discipline is not reaching schools.[12] Given the continued—and regular—use of behavioral interventions, it seems surprising that there is not more discussion about how to use them effectively. In my discussions with teachers and counselors in many different settings, remarkably few have been offered training in this area or even provided guidance in how to think about such interventions; that is, they are expected to understand them and know how to implement something akin to a formal plan. Opportunities for training and ongoing consultation are clearly needed.

In exploring the need for adapting theory to practice, a major thesis of this book is that current models of behavioral intervention would be enhanced by linking them with the mental health community's traditional commitment to systems thinking, relationship building, and value-oriented practice. *Systems thinking* means, essentially, that we try to appreciate all the influences on a child's behavior. Along with the child's innate temperament and his history of relationships with family, school, and community, we also need to make sense of relevant environmental contributors. A child living in severe poverty without adequate nutrition or health care is likely to appear more distracted than other children. Similarly, children living amid traumatizing conditions are often less able to calm themselves or respond confidently to new challenges. A behavioral intervention will not alter such life circumstances.

The notion of *value-oriented practice* is an extension of this idea. While we must continually encourage children to behave responsibly, their need for support should override the immediate inclination to punish them when they cannot. There is room for punishment when this is warranted, but it is not a starting point. These values—that context matters and that trusted relationships are a foundation of children's healthy development—imply a different understanding and way of being than the underlying assumption that a child's behavioral problems should be fixed solely by the child himself. A core value, as well, is that some numbers of children need to learn the *skills* of behavior, and adults should participate in the effort to teach them.

How a child understands any kind of intervention, whether psychological, environmental, or medical, is crucial to its success. One might look at the notion of meaning as a kind of intervening variable; that is, we must factor it in when evaluating the outcome of a particular intervention. The intervention may have been helpful (or not), but why? From the child's own perspective, it is helpful to determine what elements he specifically found beneficial. Certainly, given the growing movement in the adult mental health field toward utilizing client satisfaction reports (Brown, Dreis, & Nace, 1999),[13] we should adapt our prevailing techniques to children. What this means, therefore, is that we might ask children how the intervention is working for them. In my many years of consulting, I have never seen this done in any kind of systematic way. Perhaps there is an overriding fear that children will simply trash the plan, especially if they are unsuccessful with it. Yet, as most therapists would acknowledge, few aspects of our interactions with children are more illuminating than hearing directly from them about their felt experiences. Behavioral interventions, if seen as supportive rather than coercive—viewing the actions we take as aiming to increase good behavior rather than just punishing the bad—should not be exempted in practice from addressing their fundamental interrelationship with the meaning children attribute to them.

This might mean, for example, that rather than lecturing children about their behavior, adults might instead try first to grasp their construction of the story. Virtually any teacher or parent is familiar with children who roll their eyes when an adult begins speaking to them. The ante is raised when trying to engage particularly challenging children, and yet they require the same approach, even when it may be harder for us as adults to apply it. Asking questions and listening openly are not contrary to letting children know that certain behaviors are unacceptable. Such conduct on the part of adults does not mean the child's version fully defines truth, but rather suggests that we need to build on the way he understands and puts language to events. In addition, the act of attentive listening provides strong modeling to children who may not otherwise experience this form of interaction. All children, whether they acknowledge it or not, need to be heard and seen. These ideas are as relevant for parents on the home front as they are for teachers and counselors.

In any behavioral model, the notion of meaning does not imply that children should necessarily understand why they act as they do. This is a difficult challenge, even for adults, and the goal should reflect the developmental abilities and needs of the child. In some instances, the relatively simple act of identifying the troublesome behaviors establishes an important foundation. In others, it is enough to demonstrate to a child the cause and effect of particular behaviors so that a beginning connection is created. For some children, clarifying patterns, such as when and in what situations certain behaviors occur, is paramount. To repeat, a working understanding of what the target behaviors mean about and for the child will determine the nature of the intervention.

The following case illustrates these ideas. Jesus, an eight-year-old boy reported by his school to be defiant and oppositional, lives in a stable family environment. An only child, he has historically shown little interest in schoolwork other than in particular areas of his own interest, especially science. He loves animals and is reportedly attentive and gentle with them, yet he is rough when playing with other children, both at school and in his neighborhood. Although Jesus is described as a bright child, he is disorganized, has difficulty following multistep directions, and struggles to figure out what others expect from him in various situations. While viewed as a behavior problem in the classroom and especially during unstructured activities such as recess, his teachers find him pleasant and agreeable during their infrequent one-to-one activities with him. When I asked Jesus about his troubles at school, he immediately blurted out that it was too loud and his eyes "hurt." My impression is that, if the question had been asked before, it was during a time when he was asked to explain (and likely defend) his behavior and could not adequately do so. The outcome was further defiance. Instead, I spoke with him when he was calm and had less need to be guarded. He offered little reflection into his behavior but did have a clear view of what was bothering him. His observations concerning his eyes and ears suggested the likelihood of sensory issues, and these are typically magnified during less structured times, when there is additional noise and visual stimulation. Rather than oppositional defiant disorder, I found myself wondering about Asperger's syndrome instead. Some of the hallmark traits were clear: poor social and pragmatic skills; sensory issues; intense preoccupation with specific topics; and little willingness to engage in what did not interest him. Further investigation into his developmental history revealed a pattern consistent with this diagnosis, including early reading (decoding) skills, relatively poor comprehension, and a perseverative (that is, highly repetitive) interest in specific toys. The purpose here is to show how a different perspective for understanding Jesus's behavior—and his own insight into his situation—was instrumental to developing new strategies for helping him in school. A year later, this is a boy who is described in much more glowing terms by the staff at his school.

The complex web of children's expectations, emotions, cognitive development, and experience impacts how they understand themselves and their behavior; Neimeier (1995) refers to this as an individual's personal knowledge system.[14] Adults' efforts to remain attuned to a child's personal knowledge system—their capacity, that is, to see the world—are central to the many preventive strategies and specific behavioral interventions offered here. Moreover, children's capacity to *act* in novel ways contributes to a different perception of who they are and the nature of their relationship to the broader world. A behavioral intervention can be instrumental in expanding the repertoire of behaviors needed to enact such a process.

FUNCTIONAL BEHAVIORAL ASSESSMENTS

An existing model for assessing behavior that merits further usage and study is known as a functional behavioral assessment (FBA). Given the new laws guiding special education and the availability of specialized (and more restrictive) placement settings, functional behavioral assessments have become increasingly common in schools. Particular prototypes have been developed and marketed for this purpose. At its core, an FBA is an attempt to make sense of behavior. An article in the *ADHD Report* (Olympia & Larsen, 2005) portrays it as an "emerging component of best school practices" in the context of assessing ADHD.[15] Crone and Horner (2003, p. xii) describe the FBA process as a "method of gathering information about situational events that predict and maintain problem behavior."[16] In many respects, therefore, the new laws—and the resulting assessment tool—are in support of the notion espoused throughout this book. The functions of specific behaviors as well as the relevant conditions that support those functions are investigated, typically followed by the use of a behavioral intervention. Ideally, any behaviors targeted by the behavior plan should be based on the findings of the FBA. When a subsequent intervention is not successful, the next step is referred to as a manifestation determination hearing, at which time the special education team decides if the child should be placed in the more restrictive setting. The team must also decide on disciplinary issues and whether a particular behavior is understood as a function of a child's disability or is, conversely, an unrelated concern that requires a disciplinary action. Thus the FBA is formally part of a legal as well as clinical sequence of events.

Returning to the case description of Jesus, an FBA addressed the question of his reported defiance and investigated possible functions of that behavior. With behavioral disorders especially, it is important to try to understand the context for the behavior. When does it occur? In what situations? Are there specific times or academic periods in which the behaviors tend to emerge? For Jesus, he was comfortable one-to-one with adults, challenging in larger group situations (especially when there were academic demands that were not intrinsically interesting to him), and even more confrontational in unstructured social situations. The discovery that he loved science and held intensive interest in other particular (and narrow) areas pointed to not only a possible diagnosis—which is not the real purpose of the FBA—but, more importantly, a set of strategies for helping him. These included such interventions as a social skills group; a structured recess; a prearranged seating assignment at lunch that paired him with peers rather than placing him at an open table with large groups of children; and a small-group academic period (in the resource room), in which he received additional time to link new learning to his areas of interest. In spite of some initial resistance by administrators, none of these interventions was exceptionally difficult for the school to implement. In the aggregate, they reflected a different way of understanding Jesus. The FBA additionally suggested a direction for structuring a behavior plan, one that focused on the goals of following directions and taking two deep breaths as a way to develop self-calming skills.

Once again, however, we need to address the question of *meaning* from children's perspective. How is the FBA conducted, and by whom? For what reason? Ultimately, the progression from FBA to behavioral intervention returns us to the larger question of whether the plan is instituted in ways that fit with the child's temperament, environment, and relational needs. Jesus' plan was successful in these areas. At times, however, FBAs are used more as technical assessment tools than as real helping mechanisms, which may fit the letter of the law but does little to enhance the child's milieu or behavioral functioning. Crone and Horner (2003), in the preface to their book,[17] allude to the *technology* of FBAs without any discussion of the relational and meaning-making aspects children attribute to them. Perhaps it is implied that relationships matter, but this needs to be spelled out in greater detail. Nonetheless, the adoption of the FBA process suggests that there is some degree of acceptance toward the notion that children reflect—through their behavior—widely different perceptions of the world, challenges, biology, and experience. Conceptually, this represents a positive step forward in the evolution of schools' thinking about difficult behavior. As Crone and Horner (2003) note, "the challenge is to embed these strategies [of positive behavioral support] in the complex and demanding culture of our schools" (p. 4).[18]

Behavioral interventions can be used as a form of assessment, a slightly different idea than that behind FBAs; that is, one might start with the plan and, over a two-week period, assess its capacity to help the child alter his behavior. This reinforces the value of attempting such an intervention because teachers are not consigning themselves to endless usage. Instead, they are agreeing to look at whether there is a resulting benefit or, even if seemingly unsuccessful in helping to change the actual behavior, useful data that might reveal further information about the child. I find scores of teachers and schools reticent to employ behavioral plans that are willing to go forward in this way.

COGNITIVE BEHAVIOR THERAPY

While the focus of this book is on the application of behavioral interventions in the context of a broader understanding of children's needs, it is useful to look briefly at the basic tenets of cognitive behavior therapy (CBT). CBT has become increasingly popular within the mental health fields because it is viewed as a well-researched and evidence-based form of practice. This therapeutic model, created and initially developed by Aaron Beck, emphasizes the child's capacity to make sense of his experience. It aims, in short, to improve the child's interpretive abilities. CBT "intervenes at the cognitive-behavioral level to influence thinking, acting, feelings, and bodily reaction patterns" (Friedberg & McClure, 2002, p. 4).[19] As such, it is a change-oriented approach to doing psychotherapy that relies less on psychological insight than active changes in thinking and behavior. In this respect, CBT builds on Wachtel's earlier work. From a theoretical perspective, it incorporates feelings and thoughts (and, as such, one's lived experience) into the stimulus-response equation. Another way of saying this is that no two people respond identically to the same situation, which implies that additional factors are involved beyond a particular event and the reaction to it. Proponents of CBT contend that it is our thoughts and emotions that mediate between the two and determine the individualized nature of our behavioral responses. It is not a stretch to suggest that thinking and feeling are affected by the character of our interpersonal relationships, both past and current.

While the model has been criticized at times for ignoring the salience of the relationship between client and therapist, more recent theorists (Drisko, 1999) have attempted to address the importance of this as an integral factor in creating the conditions for change.[20] Drisko, for example, points out how essential it is to engage with clients and develop an empathic relationship before launching into an exploration of their thoughts and feelings. People are not robots. And children, who rarely come voluntarily to therapy because they are either brought by caregivers or sent by schools or court systems, will simply shut down if not given adequate time to establish a comfortable connection. Any clinician who has worked with adolescents is more than familiar with the process. The quality of relationship matters in any model of therapy and, for that matter, in any important interactions between child and adult. CBT, which is often presented as a data-driven and scientifically validated model, is not exempted from this basic and deeply human reality.

Clearly the feedback to a struggling student concerning his performance on a behavior plan could be construed as an informal type of CBT since its purpose is to help the child develop more effective strategies to regulate himself. At its center, CBT is a problem-solving approach. Ultimately, the capacity to self-regulate is rooted in one's ability to observe, understand, and anticipate one's own behavior; both CBT and formal behavioral interventions can be instrumental in helping to develop the skills needed in such a process. For example, a child who begins to understand that his tendency to overreact to small slights lends itself to other children actively trying to set him off can develop a different thought process that intercedes between the stimulus (the teasing) and his rageful reaction (the response). He can improve his level of skill at investigating this kind of scenario and generating alternative behavioral responses such as walking away. Meichenbaum (2003), an influential cognitive-behavioral psychologist, illustrates these theoretical notions clearly, especially in his contention that behavioral issues and, ultimately, the entire spectrum of mental health problems should be operationalized—and addressed—in problem-solving terms rather than with critical and moral judgments about an individual's worthiness.[21] If it is going to be effective, feedback to children using behavioral interventions should follow these principles of CBT.

THE IMPORTANCE OF RELATIONSHIP BUILDING

It should be clear from everything said up to now and the array of strategies described in the next chapter that relationships matter. All of the recommended interventions are less powerful—and less efficient—without an overarching awareness of and concern for the relational bonds involved in making them effective. Research by Hubble, Duncan, and Miller (1999), although focusing primarily on the specifics of psychotherapy, supports the essential nature of the relationship role as a critical variable in creating and maintaining the conditions for change.[22] Their research closely examines the factors associated with success in psychotherapy. A key finding is that the relationship between therapist and client explains much in the way of whether treatment is successful. In research terms, it explains a certain amount of variance. These investigators found that, aside from the client's own characteristics and experiences, the therapeutic relationship was the most salient feature in determining treatment outcome. Given the strength of such a finding, one might extrapolate that children's emotional and behavioral success could be at least partially be accounted for by the nature of their relationships with significant adults in school.

While therapists tend to emphasize, pay attention to, and reflect on their interpersonal relationships with clients, there is substantively less discussion of this issue within schools. In spite of the many protests that schools are not therapeutic settings, I would argue that they serve as such. In lieu of other adult relationships during the more than 30 hours per week children spend at school, the quality of interactions with teachers, counselors, principals, and other adults in the school would seem necessarily intertwined with how children understand and conduct themselves.

Marzano (2003), in fact, offers research-based support for the notion that teacher-student relationships are linked to successful behavior management in general.[23] He contends that teachers who are able to show students that they are in control of the class (referred to in rather strong terms as *dominance*), while at the same time displaying *cooperation* and interest in their students, are most effective. This language can be reframed to mean that a teacher's capacity to both set consistent limits and remain attuned to the children in his or her class are necessary ingredients for avoiding or lessening behavioral issues.

Similarly, Poulsen (2001) raises the issue of what he calls *affect attunement* among teachers and their students.[24] Like Siegel and Hartzell (2003; their work is discussed below),[25] he addresses the notion of intersubjective relatedness, which, in simpler terms, has to do with the degree and quality of relationships. Poulsen's study reinforces the thesis that strong relationships promote better learning. While some of these findings might seem obvious on the surface, there has been little empirical support for them. And, surprisingly, there is generally very limited discussion of relational issues in school settings. It may be that school staff—who are busy from the moment they step into their buildings—assume that good relationships are an *effect* of good student behavior, rather than a contributing cause. Rarely do I hear during a consultation the question of how adults can improve their relationships with children, especially when a situation is escalated. More frequently, the immediate focus is on what the child needs to do differently to improve his behavior.

The recent—and beneficial—move to establish mentoring programs in various middle school settings can be understood as further credence for emphasizing strong adult-child relationships. The idea that children should be *known* by adults, in a forum that allows for an open exchange of ideas and problem-solving approaches, suggests that there is some level of recognition for the need to build and sustain relationships. Mentoring, although it is set up programmatically in disparate ways, is essentially a small-group check-in for children with a single adult in which they discuss various topics relevant to their experience of school. A number of children have commented—consistent with the observations of many teachers I have interviewed—that it is the sole time in school that they feel heard.

Clinicians and educators fundamentally adhere to the ethic that safe and nurturing relationships are critical to children's healthy development. Yet curiously little is known about how the *lack* of engagement ultimately impacts them, especially given the number of lonely, isolated children we see every day in school settings. While there is a clinical diagnosis that categorizes children with severely disrupted histories of attachment, it does little to illuminate their experience. Often, these are children who present with a poorly developed ability to regulate their mood, behavior, and level of attention. Yet children's behaviors cannot truly be understood as standing apart from their social context.

Siegel and Hartzell's (2003) writing on attachment and its impact on the brain,[26] which builds on an earlier literature concerning the concept of attachment (the work of John Bowlby, for example), supplies a convincing rationale for entitling children to meaningful, attentive, and sustaining relationships. In essence, Siegel and Hartzell contend that a strong relationship (a so-called secure attachment) can alter the basic neurology of children's brains, allowing them to build new skills and strengths. Siegel and Hartzell (2003, p. 103) refer to what they call the ABCs of attachment.[27] These are (1) *attunement,* or "aligning your own internal state with those of your children. Often accomplished by the contingent sharing of nonverbal signals"; (2) *balance,* through which "your children attain balance of their body, emotions, and states of mind through attunement with you"; and (3) *coherence,* or "the sense of integration that is acquired by your children through your relationship with them in which they are able to come to feel both internally integrated and interpersonally connected to others."

These three components, described in complex neurological terms, speak simply to the need for children to be loved and understood. Siegel and Hartzell are careful to point out that the conditions for these different aspects of relationship can arise later in childhood and are not required early on for healthy development to occur. They view them as critical factors for developing resilience, the capacity to withstand and cope with difficult life circumstances. Similarly, Fraser's (1997) research into the topic of resilience offers empirical support for the critical role of a strong connection with a trusted adult.[28] There is a consistency to these findings that further reinforces the importance of relationship building between children and their adult caregivers.

In a number of situations, I have witnessed children thought to be unreachable who, through a powerful relationship with a teacher or counselor, begin to chart a more positive course. In their novel conception, Siegel and Hartzell tie together the architecture of the brain and a child's experience of the social world. Overall, this literature reveals that children's healthy relationships with adults are more than a humane undertaking; they are crucial to the formation and nurturing of their developmental capabilities.

As a result of such new research and thinking, we are witness to the beginning of perhaps another pendulum shift that can guide our understanding of how to better formulate mental health interventions for children. A recent book (Robb, 2006) elaborates on the so-called relational revolution in adult psychology that is opposed to traditional views embedded in a perception of human beings as independent and, to an extent, relatively unaffected by social connections.[29] Robb draws on the work of three pioneering psychologists to illustrate these ideas, including Carol Gilligan, Jean Baker Miller, and Judith Lewis Herman. In essence, she argues that their findings demonstrate a stronger direction for psychology, one that builds on our evolving progress in valuing the influence of social connectedness and the significance of relationship building.

Another way of understanding this perceptible shift is that medication has ruled for some time as the so-called hard science treatment approach, with psychotherapy viewed as an ostensibly softer form of intervention. Yet, with health-related "black box" warnings recommended for both antidepressants and stimulants, there is a renewed emphasis on developing effective nonmedical approaches. Similarly, behavioral interventions have been interpreted as objective and data driven, while the notion of relationships with children has been seen as vague and thus secondary. But given the compelling findings that psychotherapy—the relationship in the room—can change brain structure, relationship-oriented strategies should no longer be viewed as secondary interventions. While not a replacement for medication, they should be seen as influential in and of themselves. At the same time, strong social connections must be understood as critical contributors to the success of behavioral interventions; that is, these are not separate and distinct practices, but rather interrelated factors. The biopsychosocial approach, in theory, reflects exactly this idea in terms of clinical practice.

With all the emphasis placed here on relationship building, it seems especially important to note that, in the real world, no one is perfect at this. Some of the literature on the subject of attunement seems to imply that adults must be flawlessly and continually aligned with children's emotional needs, no matter how much those needs might shift and change. Any parent or teacher, no matter how sensitive or caring an individual, can tell you that this simply is not possible. Full attunement is an ideal. Actual relationships fall on a continuum between the lack of engagement and this conception of complete attunement, with most falling somewhere within the middle of these two poles. The point is that, as adults, we need to be mindful of what we contribute to our relationships with children and explore ways to deepen them. It is an ongoing effort. We make mistakes, have bad days, and can be brought down by illness or difficult life events. Sometimes we set limits that children do not like. At other times, in a busy classroom, the needs of many children can overwhelm even our most genuine attempts to help each individual. I see too many parents, teachers, and counselors who beat themselves up because of a temporary rupture in their relationship with a child. What needs to be sustained is the willingness and effort to stay in the relationship, especially in terms of children who struggle in so many areas of their lives. Many children I see will look at whether an adult *tries*. And they are greatly—if not necessarily outwardly—appreciative of adults who apologize for mistakes they make on their end.

Similarly, not every child is grateful or trusting of adults who attempt to connect with them. As a Massachusetts Advocates for Children (Cole, O'Brien, Gadd, Ristuccia, Wallace, & Gregory, 2005) publication states, "the school setting can be a battleground in which traumatized children's assumptions of the world as a dangerous place sabotage their ability to develop constructive relationships with nurturing adults. Unfortunately, many traumatized children adopt behavioral coping mechanisms that can frustrate educators and evoke exasperated reprisals, reactions that both strengthen expectations of confrontation and danger and reinforce a negative self-image" (p. 32).[30]

It is truly a challenge to avoid personalizing a child's anger or betrayal, and yet this is exactly what is required in some circumstances. Traumatized children can be expert at figuring out how to keep adults from becoming close to them since this serves to preserve their sense of safety; that is, they need a certain degree of distance to maintain their mask of security. Among adults, the willingness and sensitivity to appreciate this reality, and the capacity to understand the ways in which trauma and different mental health issues can affect children's behaviors and their ability to trust, underlie such a challenge. The feedback process as part of a behavioral approach can help in this endeavor. If the intervention is implemented effectively, the consistency and predictability inherent to regular feedback can be used both to build a level of trust and to repair it when there has been a rupture in the relationship. This notion of feedback and how it works will be discussed more fully in chapter 5.

INCLUDING PARENTS IN SCHOOLS

I have already alluded to the role of parents, but this subject deserves a closer look. Since the current chapter emphasizes the need to deepen our understanding of children's behavior amid their development of meaningful relationships with adults, it makes sense to explore parents' place in all this. Certainly there is tremendous guilt and worry that parents reveal to us around children who struggle with school, behavior, and their overall success in life. Yet there is sometimes a sense in schools that parents are fully to blame for the misbehaviors of their children. And, to be fair, there are scenarios in which this appears to be at least partially true. Parents who are neglectful or abusive, or those who point a finger at the school every time there is a problem, do not aid in setting up a dynamic that supports children's healthy development. On the other hand, I find that parents can be held accountable for the same bewildering behaviors in their children that teachers and school administrators struggle with; that is, there are plenty of children who confuse and confound their parents.

It was not all that long ago that family therapists began to recognize that parental depression or anxiety may be a *result* of children's struggles. The default position was that parents were responsible for their children in entirety, with the related assumption that children merely reflected their parents' beliefs and attitudes. We are all familiar with the adage that the apple does not fall far from the tree, and this is certainly true in some situations. Many developmental disorders have been found to have a genetic component, but that does not mean that parental *fault* should be part of the equation. A large number of children have developmental disorders that show up nowhere else in a family, and the perplexing behaviors of children with, for example, Tourette's syndrome can be as baffling and upsetting to their parents as to anyone else. In chapter 2, we look more closely at, among other childhood disorders, Asperger's syndrome and ADHD, and both of these entail children—and sometimes parents—who challenge schools and, subsequently, our sense of how the school-parent contract should work. The point here is that we should attempt to be aware of the biases many of us carry into our work in schools. Just as we need an individualized approach to understanding children's behavior, we should adopt a similar perspective in terms of their parents. This is neither fast nor easy but is worth it over the long run.

These ideas also lend themselves to the related question of what kinds of support schools should offer to parents. There is an honest and at times heated debate about this. On one end of the spectrum are schools in which the predominant view seems to be that, given limited resources, teachers and other staff have more than enough to do and that school should be geared solely to academic pursuits; that is, education is viewed in narrow, somewhat traditional terms. While there may be some deference to the idea of working partnerships with parents, there is in effect a firewall between the school and the rest of the community. On the other side, some districts view their schools as fundamentally a community enterprise (Dryfoos, 1994).[31] In a number of urban districts, schools serve a number of community functions, including the provision of formal and informal supports for parents. One of the selling points of the growing number of charter schools, I believe, is that, along with their self-made promise of turning out higher standardized test scores, many of these schools emphasize a strong working relationship with parents. There is no simple answer to how to deliver services to families—this has been an enduring and vexing social policy question—but it seems evident that an ongoing discussion, one that includes parents as an important constituency, must continue to take place.

THE ROLE OF MENTAL HEALTH PROVIDERS

The role of mental health providers is another question that frequently comes up for discussion in schools. Since a primary thesis of this book is that mental health issues underlie many behavioral problems that show up in schools, it leads to the obvious conclusion that more mental health supports are required. As any parent knows who seeks services for a child, there is often a patchwork of available services; the primary care physician is in one place, a psychiatrist in another, and a therapist may be located in a third, none of whom may be in contact with the school or one another. Coordination of services is essential when working with children, and schools are often left out of the loop in terms of information that might be beneficial if shared with relevant staff. Parents are at times exhausted and frustrated by this lack of coordination, and it is beyond the scope of what any school psychologist or counselor can handle. Teachers, too, may be disturbed by the lack of communication with the mental health system since they are—especially during the elementary school years, when they have the same children in their classrooms virtually all day—the frontline providers who can report in some detail about the child's behavior and, subsequently, the value of any interventions.

As further evidence for these notions, Rappaport, Flaherty, and Hauser (2006) studied 33 severely disruptive children with a history of threatened or actual violence.[32] They found that many of these children lack appropriate treatment for their mental health needs. Similarly, a lack of cohesiveness was apparent in terms of the services they did receive. In sum, these researchers pointed to the "intensity of services" these children require if we are to respond more successfully to their "complexities of need" and help them adjust to the demands of school and growing up. There are ways to do this, but they entail a commitment to employing mental health services that are coordinated, child- and family-centered, and able to address the whole child. Well-designed behavioral interventions are one piece of this larger puzzle. In addition, there must be greater willingness to pay for mental services that are preventive rather than reactive.

On the basis of the thinking outlined in this chapter, what strategies are therefore useful for helping children with their behavior, and similarly, from where do these strategies arise? Scratching beneath the surface is challenging but necessary work, especially at a time when diagnostic labels and short-term (often medically based) interventions are so dominant. Given current mandates, the idea of slowing down to reflect on our practice approaches seems almost quaint, yet it is imperative if we are to improve the quality of our work with children.

Chapter 2

COMMON MENTAL HEALTH DIAGNOSES: HOW THEY IMPACT CHILDREN

In this chapter, an overview of several mental health diagnoses will be provided. These six diagnostic categories were selected because they are generally associated with children who present with challenging behaviors. Moreover, the behavioral *characteristics* of these diagnoses are intertwined with the kinds of thinking and intervention approaches depicted throughout this book.

ASPERGER'S SYNDROME

While the American Psychiatric Association's (2000) *Diagnostic and Statistical Manual,* 4th edition (known as *DSM–IV–TR,* or "text revision") describes a particular set of characteristics, children with this diagnosis present in divergent ways.[33] The common theme is social concerns since children with Asperger's syndrome (AS) typically have difficulty in understanding social cues and making connections around shared interests. Managing anxiety is a paramount concern. The diagnosis became official only as recently as 1994 when the most recent edition of the *DSM* was published, although the issues were identified by Hans Asperger, an Austrian physician, during the 1940s. Because so many individuals with AS look typical in appearance and have both high intelligence and the capacity to articulate their interests, there is at times the belief that they are simply manipulative or lazy, rather than struggling with an identified set of real-life issues.

There are almost always concerns with pragmatic speech, which is linked to the interpersonal world since it encompasses the broad realm of social language. The effort to understand the nuances and idioms of the English language, to make sense of the subtle messages from another person and respond appropriately, and even to comprehend what others find interesting or important, is draining for many children with AS and leaves them stressed and less available for the other demands of school. Furthermore, the rigidity around rules and what's fair often found in children with AS exacerbates their social difficulties. In addition, there may be word-finding problems, especially when the child is experiencing increased stress. As such, demanding that the child explain himself during a difficult time will only lead to a shutdown or, more likely, a blowup. Receptively, these are children who often report that they feel overwhelmed by an abundance of verbal language. I know an adolescent girl who describes the experience of sitting amid a stream of chatter as an "onslaught" and one in which she has to shut down to survive; all talk is reduced to white noise, like the machine used in many professionals' offices to disguise private conversations. She simply is unable to process large amounts of speech, and this is not an unusual occurrence for people of all ages with AS.

Children with AS typically experience one or more forms of overstimulation. While school staff are often aware of the issue of loud noise, there may be sensitivity to bright lights, movement in the visual field (which describes, for example, what happens at recess, in the lunchroom, and during hall passing), certain smells, and particular tastes and textures. Cognitively, they tend to be self-directed learners, with an intense interest in what intrigues them and limited concern for what does not. Given this, it is not surprising that a number of children with AS choose to be home schooled, though this can deprive them of needed opportunities for social learning. Demonstrating what they know is a paramount academic issue as it is a regular occurrence that I hear of children who seem to comprehend more than they display. Parents frequently describe children who "know it at home" but not in school, which is based on a few different factors. One, anxiety tends to inhibit their capacity to produce. Second, handwriting is notoriously difficult, and teacher expectations for this often lead to overall fatigue; many individuals with AS have fine motor (as well as gross motor) issues. Finally, given the finding that people with AS may struggle with comprehending the thinking and interests of others (which is known, more formally, as *theory of mind*), some children simply do not understand why they need to show someone else what they know. For example, one high school student with AS emphatically told me that he knows geometry and should not have to write out theorems because he expects that the teacher should know how to do math as well.

The rudeness and defiant behavior sometimes observed in children with AS is an issue confronting many schools and parents. While non-compliance or aggression is never a welcome occurrence, and the diagnosis of AS should serve as an explanation rather than an excuse for these behaviors, it is imperative that we attempt to make sense of such behavior and develop strategies for countering it. Generally, rudeness occurs when children have accumulated too much anxiety and cannot either identify an impending problem or enact a strategy to respond effectively to it. I see this more as a performance (skills deficit) issue than purposeful behavior. The lack of awareness that not uncommonly accompanies the display of such behavior—and sometimes the resigned sadness afterward, indicating the child's sense of helplessness in this area—suggests that there is little intention behind such acts. An emphasis on prevention, by attempting to preclude the individual's reaching his threshold of tolerance, is the objective. Once that threshold is reached, teachers, counselors, and parents may be thrust into managing a crisis.

John, a 13-year-old seventh grader diagnosed with AS, is bright, self-motivated as a learner, and invested in finding out everything he can about science. He is also perseverative about topics that interest him, aloof toward those that do not, and highly anxious. Like many children with AS, he was initially categorized as having ADHD, but his degree of social awkwardness and related inability to recognize social cues became increasingly apparent as he moved up in grade level during elementary school. Both parents report a similar history of anxiety, at times debilitating for his father. Although John earned strong grades in school, he was intermittently rude to teachers and peers, unable to tolerate much in the way of frustration, and a mess when he got home from school. A behavior plan that distributed points for positive behavior and took them away for problematic behavior had been unsuccessful because John perseverated on the possibility of losing them. He was sent to the assistant principal for rude comments, which at times led to a full-blown rage. My impression is that his teachers perceived these comments as intentional and a result of entitled behavior rather than based on his diagnosis of AS. It was only when we compiled data indicating the pattern of these comments—always in high-stress social or classroom situations—that school staff began to view him in a different way. This allowed for the employment of a new set of intervention strategies, including scheduled

breaks to reduce anxiety and a revision of his behavior plan (consistent
with the model depicted later in this book). Social skills training and
a short-term, family-based intervention to identify and manage anxiety,
both of which were undertaken outside of school, were also instituted.
Progress has come in spurts, but John is currently functioning more
successfully—and comfortably—in school.

It is worth noting that children with nonverbal learning disabilities
(NVLD) often present with similar traits. These are children who typically have difficulty understanding social cues, generalizing what they
know, and making meaning out of an array of facts; that is, it can be
a struggle to see the forest for the trees. Such children need to hear it
(and say it) rather than see it or do it, and thus language abilities are more
strongly developed than performance skills. The fact that these children
need to use verbal rehearsal of material sometimes leads to difficulty in
the classroom because they are told to be quiet, and their inability to
do so is perceived as a behavioral issue, rather than as a learning need.
In the area of reading, decoding skills are typically fine, which masks
their struggles with comprehension. Like children with AS, those with
NVLD often exhibit poor motor planning and are therefore clumsy and
easily fatigued by physical tasks. The research on NVLD is emerging as we are just recently starting to make better sense of it. Much
more is known about children with language-based learning disabilities.
NVLD is categorized as a learning disability rather than a psychiatric
diagnosis, and it certainly has an impact on children in schools as well
as at home. For more information, excellent resources include Pamela
Tanguay (2002) and Sue Thompson (1997), both of whom have published readable books on the topic.[34,35]

It is equally important to note that AS is on the *spectrum* of autistic
disorders. In the *DSM–IV,* this spectrum is lumped together within a
category known as pervasive developmental disorder, although the different diagnoses are frequently referred to as autism spectrum disorders
(ASD). AS is seen as the highest form, a slight variation of what is
known as high-functioning autism (HFA). The difference is based on
whether or not, developmentally, the child displays essentially normal
language skills. Severe autism, including Rett's disorder (which primarily affects girls) and childhood disintegrative disorder, are at the other
end of the continuum. Cognitive delays are a facet of the more severe
manifestations of autism.

With the explosion in prevalence rates, most school staff have at least
a passing familiarity with autism spectrum disorders, even if not trained
in their complexities. Data based on recent brain studies indicate that

people with autism have larger brains than neurotypical people but that there are fewer neural connections, especially in the parts of the brain that contribute to social understanding and reasoning. Physiologically, then, there appear to be some genuine differences between people on the spectrum and those who are not. The burgeoning research into ASDs also reveals that there is a strong genetic component. The question of what fully *causes* autism, however, has not been definitively answered.

For further discussion of AS, including its characteristic traits, there are a number of excellent print and online resources. A good starting point for the former is Tony Attwood's (1998) *Asperger's Syndrome: A Guide for Parents and Professionals,* although many newer books have surpassed it in terms of detail and specific issues related to the disorder.[36] The Online Asperger's Support and Information Service (OASIS; http://www.udel.edu/bkirby/asperger) provides updated articles, references, and relevant information.

ANXIETY

Although the concept of anxiety can be operationalized as a set of specific (and sometimes overlapping) disorders, the broad notion of anxiety is understood to be the most prevalent psychiatric condition in this country (Chansky, 2004).[37] Given the sobering finding that the majority of adults impacted by anxiety disorders report that their symptoms began during childhood, it seems clear that a closer look at this topic is needed when addressing the issue of children's behavior and their related need for support. Consistent with the depiction in *DSM–IV,* Foxman (2004) offers the following subtypes:[38]

generalized anxiety disorder (or overanxious disorder)

avoidant disorders

phobic disorders

posttraumatic stress disorder (PTSD)

panic disorder

obsessive-compulsive disorder (OCD, which includes trichotillomania, or hair pulling)

anxiety associated with medical conditions

substance-induced anxiety disorder

separation anxiety disorder, diagnosed solely in children.

As in cases of AS, anxiety tends to be cumulative, rather than an either-or phenomenon. Given this, it may not be clear when children are experiencing anxiety, especially because they do not necessarily appear anxious or report symptoms consistent with the way adults do so. Often overlooked is the notion that anxiety stems from different sources: while Chansky denotes four areas, a more simplified way of understanding this is that there are both environmental and biological contributors. The former includes parenting style, life experiences, a stressful school situation, and so on. The latter, less often recognized and discussed, takes into account the child's temperament, developmental course, and physiological predisposition. Some children are simply more prone to high anxiety, regardless of what occurs in their broader environment of home, school, and friends. Or, in a related way, the same set of events that they can tolerate one day may lead to a meltdown on the next.

As noted throughout this book, children's behavior can describe their affective or feeling states. Many children with high anxiety present as edgy, irritable, angry, and/or fatigued. To me, they usually seem joyless while in the throes of their anxiety. Seen from this perspective, it makes sense that children with unremitting anxiety would present in such ways since they are hindered by their ongoing negative experience. I had a case a number of years ago involving a boy in early adolescence who became suicidal due to an extreme case of panic disorder. It was not until a combination of cognitive behavior therapy, relaxation strategies, and short-term medication was in place that his suicidality and negative behavior decreased.

A fuller example concerns Alec, 12 years old and in sixth grade, who presented as a generally good-natured child through fifth grade when, suddenly and without any clear reason, he became increasingly unhappy and defiant. Not a particularly introspective or reflective child, it was challenging for his parents and teachers—and family physician—to make sense of what was happening for him. A psychologist initially diagnosed him with a so-called incipient oppositional disorder, but this did not resonate for the adults who know Alec well. One of his teachers at the middle school—he had transitioned out of the elementary school for sixth grade—observed that he seemed clenched and tense when called on to speak in class. Asked directly about this, Alec told his father that he was not sleeping well, "worried about everything," and was continually frightened that he would fail in school. This is a boy who has excellent family and school supports, so it did not take long to follow the story along to its natural conclusion: a mixed case of generalized anxiety and panic disorder. Although there was some family history of anxiety, it was not compelling, and given Alec's gender, overall competence (both as a student and a skilled athlete), and hard-charging approach to things, no one had thought to explore anxiety as an underlying cause for his changed behavior and affect. It is not unusual for children to manifest developmental changes during middle school, and for Alec, he had no language to describe his experience. He also, apparently, was ashamed of his "weakness" and had not wanted to talk to anyone about it. Once treatment for anxiety was begun, which included individual therapy, parent coaching, and consultation to the school, Alec made good progress. A footnote to the case is that he recently experienced a reemergence of high anxiety, but the additional supports were renewed, and it dissipated more quickly than during the initial occurrence.

Good sources for learning more about anxiety are plentiful, but a few will be noted here. Tamar Chansky's *Freeing Your Child from Anxiety,* Paul Foxman's *The Worried Child,* and Edna Foa and Reid Wilson's (2001) *Stop Obsessing* are particularly helpful.[39] Philip Kendall's (1992) Coping Cat program is a useful treatment package.[40] David Burns's (2006) excellent self-help book *When Panic Attacks* is a manual and guide based on cognitive behavioral principles.[41] There are numerous online resources as well.

ATTENTION-DEFICIT/HYPERACTIVITY DISORDER

Although there are three subtypes of ADHD, it is typically the hyperactive-impulsive type (or the combined, which includes these traits with inattention) that brings children, usually boys, into contact with counselors and other service providers. ADHD is defined in *DSM–IV* in terms of specific behavioral criteria that reflect hyperactivity, impulsivity, and, when relevant, inattention. A child must exhibit six or more traits out of a total list of nine to be formally diagnosed as having ADHD. An issue with this classification is that there are many reasons why a child may be inattentive or impulsive, or even physically hyperactive. Without a careful assessment of the child's developmental and social history, there may be a misdiagnosis of either a false positive or false negative (Levine, 1997).[42] Noting that a child is all over the room, impulsive, and exhibiting poor attention and persistence is not sufficient for arriving at such a diagnosis, yet this is precisely what happens in some instances. More recent research (Barkley, 2005) reveals that disinhibition of behavior and a poor understanding of time (which leads to issues with time management, the capacity to put things in sequence, and the overall ability to organize oneself) are better markers for the disorder.[43] Strategies discussed later in the chapter are geared to this conceptualization of ADHD. Barkley's body of work is a good place to begin if one wishes to delve further into this topic, and there is a vast parent and professional literature concerning ADHD. *The ADHD Report,* a bimonthly newsletter edited by Barkley, offers updates on the subject along with new research findings.

An example concerns Melanie, 13 years old and attending sixth grade. Diagnosed at a young age with ADHD (the combined type, which includes inattention with both impulsivity and hyperactivity), she repeated kindergarten because she missed out on so much of that year while reportedly zooming from place to place in the classroom. Although female, there was apparently no mistaking the diagnosis in her situation. She displayed the classic signs of ADHD such as impulsive behavior, restlessness, and inattention. She also missed social cues, and this was the primary reason she was held back during the early portion of her school experience. Her parents believed that, in spite of her good intelligence, she needed an additional year to become acclimated to the demands of school and learn how to respond to rules, structure, and the burden of making sense of other children. Stimulant medication, which she began later in elementary school in spite of her parents' misgivings about using medication, was effective in reducing the core symptoms of ADHD, that is, the fidgety body, impulsive behavior, and inability either to maintain or accurately shift attention. Soon after she turned 12 years old, however, Melanie developed side effects that precluded her use of this class of medications. She was unable to sleep, was not eating, and began to have tics. As a result, she was switched to Strattera, the first nonstimulant medication approved to treat ADHD. This has had some success in combating the core symptoms, but not as much as the stimulants had contributed. Social situations have remained somewhat puzzling for her, impacting her ability to connect with other children. In addition, signs of anxiety have cropped up, which is not unusual: most children diagnosed with ADHD have at least one co-occurring diagnosis. In terms of intervention, a combination of medication, a behavioral intervention to help with her blurting out during class, a social skills training group in school, and individual therapy have helped Melanie to function more effectively and, reportedly, to feel more comfortable in school.

POSTTRAUMATIC STRESS DISORDER

Although PTSD is categorized as an anxiety disorder, it is very much an internal response to actual life events. In *DSM–IV,* it is classified in relation to the following: the individual is "exposed to a traumatic event" and the traumatic event is "persistently reexperienced" in one or more ways (including, in children, frightening dreams, repetitive play that expresses aspects of the trauma, reenactment of the traumatic events, intense psychological distress, and disorganized and agitated behavior). In addition, there is "persistent avoidance of stimuli associated with the trauma." These formal descriptors give only a vague sense of the terror experienced by children with PTSD. Many of these children have problems regulating their attention, mood, and behavior, so they are variously labeled as having ADHD, bipolar disorder, or formal behavioral disorders, such as oppositional defiant disorder or conduct disorder. Given their lack of trust, they may also be labeled with an attachment disorder. These diagnoses may describe the presenting behavior, but they do not hint at the cause. A history of trauma does not rule out the possibility that a child can subsequently present with such disorders (although the symptoms of ADHD, for example, are supposed to be evident by the age of seven), but, once again, it is imperative to be aware of their context. Why? Because such children do not typically respond well to forceful and angry directives from authority figures, and, conversely, such interventions at times can lead to larger blowups and rage reactions. Instead, it is—among other interventions—the ability to provide calm nurturance while maintaining clear limits and consequences that helps these children. Thus, as this book consistently asserts, enhancing our understanding of where a problem stems from can help us refine our intervention approaches.

My practice is filled with children who have experienced trauma. A composite illustration of this is the following: Carla is a nine-year-old third grader born to a severely drug-addicted father and a mother with a history of her own physical and sexual abuse. In spite of the mother's experience, she has worked hard to parent Carla and her younger brother, providing them with both financial and emotional support. There was a frightening period of domestic violence that Carla witnessed, following previous intermittent periods of belligerent behavior, as her father—who is now prohibited from any contact with the family—became paranoid and physically assaultive toward his wife. The final incident was one in which Carla called the police to request help for her mother, who ended up in the hospital with broken bones and other serious injuries. It was this event that culminated in the father's imprisonment and a subsequent restraining order. As a young child, Carla experienced guilt and responsibility over this series of events, as she reported that she was to blame "for everything." While she was generally a helpful contributor at home with her younger sibling, her behavior toward her mother and people at school became angry, rage driven, and, at times, aggressive. Her academic performance began to spiral downward as she seemed unable to concentrate and uncaring about her schoolwork. A behavioral intervention that aimed to reduce aggression had no positive impact as the inability to earn rewards and the corresponding loss of privileges infuriated Carla to the point of explosion. Events reached their nadir when she tried to hit the principal after he "lectured" her about her behavior. As a result, she was suspended from school.

This is not a unique story. Too many children have witnessed violence or have been the direct victims of it. In Carla's case, there was much to work with because her mother was a compassionate influence in spite of the lack of extended family supports. Nonetheless, Carla's behavior was a legitimate concern. Fortunately, the school was open to being flexible and eager to help this child. After the suspension, they reassigned a paraprofessional to work with her for a segment of the day and to provide her with one-to-one instruction outside the classroom. A renewed focus on helping Carla to predict what would happen during the school day was also instituted. If she felt that she needed to leave the classroom, there was a prearranged safe spot for her to go. Initially, she needed prompts to go there, but fairly quickly, she began to identify when it was important for her to request this (simply by raising her hand and leaving—she was not required to put language to this need). Short but regular meetings with the school counselor were arranged, along with regular check-ins with other adults in the building. It was only after these interventions were in place that a behavioral plan was again instituted, this time with better results. Over time, Carla showed good progress in her ability to maintain her behavior. Things do not always turn out nearly this well for children with trauma histories, but it was the combination of family and school supports along with Carla's own innate skills that contributed to her success.

There is an emerging literature concerning children and PTSD. Greenwald's work, especially his *Child Trauma Handbook* (2005), is a good place to begin in terms of learning about treatment approaches for children who have experienced trauma.[44] Another resource is Silva's (2004) *Posttraumatic Stress Disorders in Children and Adolescents.*[45] *Helping Traumatized Children Learn* is an additional guide written for a wider audience, including teachers and other school personnel. Other researchers/writers who have made significant contributions include van der Kolk and Terr. Still, there remains much that we do not yet know about how to help traumatized children, and further research is needed.

DEPRESSION

Without delving into an elaborate description of this category, what is important to note is that depression in children is sometimes manifested through irritable behavior and a kind of edginess of mood. Similar to the discussion of anxiety, children simply do not demonstrate the disorder in the way that adults tend to expect—even though many adults also display depression in these same ways. I have seen a number of examples of children who were struggling mightily in school and, when sent for a clinical evaluation, the resultant finding of depression was a surprise for staff. Culturally, we seem to assume that depressed individuals will look sad and act blue. Many do. But others do not, and this certainly is not uncommon among children. Interventions for depression, such as individual and family therapy, medication, time with a school counselor, assertiveness training (this skill is often lacking among people with depression), and exercise, all may aid in reducing the presenting problems. The child's use of illegal drugs should be assessed, and if warranted, substance abuse treatment may be indicated. Suicidal thinking/planning must also be evaluated.

Teaching a child to recognize his own mood states and take preventive steps before becoming agitated (and acting on this anger) can be a difficult but highly rewarding task when it is successful. The ability to reflect on one's own behavior and appraise the reactions of others arises at widely different ages and reflects a number of child-specific factors. Even when it does not immediately work, therefore, the effort can help depressed children build a foundation that ultimately supports the emergence of such strategies. Sometimes children need to be cued to take the necessary steps such as leaving class if their agitation is rising. A trusting relationship in the classroom goes a long way toward enhancing the likelihood that this will occur. School counselors and teachers should work collaboratively in this endeavor, though the groundwork for such a psychoeducational approach is typically undertaken by those with formal mental health training.

For example, Josh is a nine-year-old third grader whose sudden changes in behavior mystified his teachers and parents. At times a sweet, almost shy boy, his tendency was to withdraw quietly when academic demands became too much for him or when he felt overwhelmed by social stressors. Recently—and out of the blue—he began to act defiantly both at home and, especially, in school. At these times, he appeared angry and agitated, with a kind of why-even-bother-at-all attitude toward adults. While he maintained his peer relationships for the most part, some children were confused and intimidated by his outbursts. Josh had seen a counselor a year or so earlier as a result of some indications of anxiety, much of which appeared to be in relation to discord between his parents. A brief intervention, both individual and family based, had alleviated these issues. As new concerns emerged, there were questions about what was going on for this boy.

While observing him in the classroom, it was apparent that Josh had limited ability to ask for help when he needed it; as a third grader, the teacher was now less likely to approach him to ask what he might need. As such, his behavior revealed a child who was stuck in a sort of predictable but unfortunate cycle: he did not ask for help, became upset that it was not offered, and then acted in an oppositional way because he was angry and, seemingly, felt powerless to change his situation. Positive responses, logical consequences, threats to remove privileges, and trips to the principal's office had no impact on his behavior. To me, his depression was evident: agitation, moodiness, a certain do-to-me-what-you-want attitude all suggested a boy dealing with depression. Once this formulation was in place, the interventions that followed brought about an almost immediate change. His teacher, who was concerned for Josh and willing to try anything, now approached him on a consistent basis to check in and explore whether he needed assistance. She also spent considerable time attempting to give him a language for asking for help. At those times when it appeared that he was escalating, she would offer him a face-saving out that they had developed together. For a time, Josh left the room often to take on tasks helpful to the classroom. His leaving, therefore, was now framed as help, rather than punishment. For the most part, he was able to respond successfully to such a strategy, though certainly not all the time. In addition, he was offered five sessions with the school counselor to explore ways to recognize his internal state and develop alternative approaches to becoming escalated. Finally, he is on a waiting list to see a child psychiatrist to investigate the possibility of medication. In general, though, his behavior is much improved, and the strong connection with his teacher is clearly part of what works well. In a scenario such as this one, it is the mood issues that predominate, and the strategies devoted to helping with those are more effective than any single form of reactive behavioral intervention or consequence.

Many sources for understanding childhood depression, written for parents as well as professionals, are available. Merrell's (2001) workbook,

Helping Students Overcome Depression and Anxiety, is an excellent resource.[46] *Lonely, Sad, and Angry,* by Goldstein and Ingersoll (2001), is another.[47]

BEHAVIORAL DISORDERS (OPPOSITIONAL DEFIANT DISORDER AND CONDUCT DISORDER)

According to the *DSM–IV,* oppositional defiant disorder is defined in terms of a pattern of "negativistic, hostile, and defiant behavior" that lasts for at least six months, is more frequent than would be expected from a child of that age and developmental level, and impairs functioning. Conduct disorder is a more severe manifestation of the same spectrum of concerns that involves aggression to people and animals, destruction of property, deceitfulness or theft, and/or serious violations of rules. In other words, there is a serious level of violent and/or antisocial behavior. Again, these characteristics describe behaviors but do not explain their context. There is little argument that children with these diagnoses, especially the latter, can create serious challenges for schools, families, court systems, and other service providers. Given this, it becomes an imperative mission to try to make sense of the behaviors. For example, children who have been traumatized by sexual or physical abuse may develop conduct disorders in a way that reflects or reenacts their experience of trauma. As this book notes, a child's personal history does not validate antisocial behavior, but it does help to explain it and therefore opens up various interventions that can be attempted.

As an example, Bill, age 15, arrived at a new high school for his sophomore year diagnosed with conduct disorder, bipolar disorder, and ADHD, along with questions about a reactive attachment disorder (RAD). This trio of labels implies certain behavioral characteristics such as moodiness, poor frustration tolerance, impulsivity, and a severe lack of ability or willingness to follow basic societal rules. The provisional diagnosis of RAD suggests the incapacity to develop open, trusting, and reciprocal relationships. Unfortunately, each of these descriptors fits well with Bill's specific behavioral presentation because he was in trouble as of his first day in this setting. Medications included a mood stabilizer (Depakote) and a stimulant (Concerta), though a slew of other medications had been tried previously. In essence, Bill's diagnoses reveal a major theme: the inability to regulate himself, whether in the area of mood, attention, or behavior. In addition, he did not trust relationships based on his history of early neglect, home violence, and subsequent foster care placements. Given this scenario, Bill presented many challenges. My own impression, culled from the history, is that post-traumatic stress was the underlying factor contributing to and connecting each of these descriptive diagnoses. If such a hypothesis were true, it would suggest that, until this youngster found some sense of security and safety in his environment, he would continue to present as a significant behavioral concern. Harsh penalties, a period of time in juvenile lockup, various behavioral contracts, and, as noted, a variety of medications were unhelpful in diminishing his impulsive and rageful behavior. Bill's new high school chose to take a different tack. While they recognized that their efforts might be fruitless, they were willing to commit to a period of time in which they would address his behavior as trauma based, rather than purely antisocial. This meant that he started and ended each day with the school behavioral teacher, where he reviewed both academic and behavioral expectations. The ability to anticipate his day was a new experience for him and something he gravitated to immediately. Interventions included the establishment of clear limits and consequences if he broke school rules. While such a strategy is commonly employed—and surely not new to Bill—it works most effectively when combined with other environmental and relational approaches. Used alone, it may be experienced simply as a form of "tightening the screws" (as one adolescent described it). Contact with the outside therapist and the physician prescribing his medications, typically an urgent recommendation when developing a treatment plan for complicated children, was made on behalf of Bill, which gave these providers concrete information about his functioning level and style during the school day. Furthermore, a cuing system was developed that allowed Bill to leave the classroom when needed and, unexpectedly, convinced him that school staff were not out to get him. Within the school setting, he was also provided weekly 20-minute sessions with the school counselor that focused on ways to employ self-calming techniques; a positive behavioral support plan; an additional break during the day due to his ADHD and fairly consistent degree of agitation—he used this period to organize his materials, do homework, and practice calming himself—and an open invitation to draw during class because this helped him listen more attentively to teacher instructions; that is, the act of drawing was reframed as a coping technique, rather than as a further sign of distractibility and defiant behavior. This constellation of approaches, in conjunction with a stable foster placement, contributed to a child increasingly able to maintain himself in school. While there continued to be intermittent outbursts, they were quicker to defuse, less volatile, and followed by Bill's genuine expressions of remorse. These events were described in a language that construed his behavior as impulsive rather than antisocial, a significant advance for an adolescent understood to have conduct disorder. No longer was the idea of RAD a point of discussion as Bill developed a strong bond with his foster mother and a couple of his teachers. His difficulties were by no means ended, but the improvement in his overall functioning was substantive, and there was no further discussion of sending him to an out-of-district placement. It was not any single intervention that helped Bill to turn the corner, but rather a series of coordinated strategic and relational steps coupled with a strong commitment by his team that contributed to his improved behavior.

Greene's books are a good way to understand the needs of children with severe behavioral problems. These include *The Explosive Child* (2001) and, more recently (with Ablon), *Treating Explosive Kids* (2006).[48,49] Bloomquist and Schnell's (2002) book *Helping Children with Aggression and Conduct Problems* is another resource.[50]

Each of the diagnostic categories mentioned above describes behaviors but does not define children. The *DSM* has undergone revision over the years and has vastly increased the number of diagnosable conditions. Nonetheless, anecdotal reports from educators and the mental health community suggest that the number of children with challenging developmental, learning, and behavioral needs continues to rise. As such, we know increasingly more about what is wrong with children—and how to put a label to this—but have not yet developed a coherent set of approaches for intervening meaningfully and effectively in their struggles. The following chapter is an attempt to participate in such an endeavor.

Chapter 3

TRANSLATING THE NOTIONS OF
MEANING AND RELATIONSHIP:
HELPING STRATEGIES IN ACTION
(OR THE TWENTY-SIX COMMANDMENTS)

The specific strategies discussed in this chapter reflect the idea that helping children improve their coping skills by thoughtfully forming our own guesses about the purpose and meaning of current behaviors is integral. Efforts to establish a meaningful bond with children, the commitment toward sustained dialogue, and a belief in the importance of understanding the context for behavior are critical to this. These strategies are as much art as science, as they can be employed in different ways to augment teachers' and counselors' ongoing efforts to help children with their classroom behavior.

NAME BEHAVIOR

Provide children with a clear description of their observable behavior, for example, "Joe, I can see that you're having a hard time paying attention because your legs are moving and your head is facing the back of the room—you focus best when neither one of those things is happening." This helps lay a foundation for kids who, developmentally or otherwise, cannot do this for themselves. This also builds trust and opens children to accepting adult feedback if done in a joining way. It further models the concept of exploring behavior, which reinforces self-awareness. I think of this as a way to nudge children up the developmental scale in the realm of social/emotional skills. Similarly, it makes sense to pinpoint a time when Joe is attending well and give him a description of his behavior at that moment. This can be a gift to a child who frequently finds himself in trouble as it gives him a mental picture and a language that is self-affirming.

RECOGNIZE THE POSSIBILITY OF CUMULATIVE ANXIETY

In most instances where a child has had a meltdown, schools focus on discovering a precipitating event. Even the traditional ABC charts used to track children's behavior ("antecedent, behavior, consequence") give credence to the notion that there is somehow a discrete event connected with the problem. In some instances, however, there is no single precipitating event, as many frustrated teachers will immediately acknowledge when asked about cause. Instead, some children have difficulty when their overall level of anxiety exceeds their ability to cope. In such situations, a meltdown reflects the buildup of this anxiety—the precipitating event itself may be simply the proverbial straw. This scenario is not unusual for children with generalized anxiety disorder, autistic disorders, or, more specifically, in children with AS or high-functioning autism. It is similarly true for children with other neurological disorders such as Tourette's syndrome or the low-frustration-tolerance children Greene (2001) refers to in his book *The Explosive Child*.[51] For some of these children, a fully mainstreamed program with constant social stressors (not to mention the steady stream of academic demands) challenges them in ways beyond their capacity to hold it all together. To preclude meltdowns, the school team (including the child's parents) needs to review the child's programming and identify ways to make the demands more tolerable. For instance, some children who tend to accumulate anxiety steadily during the school day need built-in break periods. This invokes both a willingness to spend the necessary time and a commitment to think proactively.

As an example, Todd, a 13-year-old boy diagnosed early on with anxiety and a mild learning disability in language processing, presented with what his teachers described as a hair-trigger temper. He was referred for consultation because the school was walking on eggshells around him. Almost all the adults, including the assistant principal in charge of discipline, reported that to confront him in even the mildest terms when he was "off" would predictably lead to a major blowup. While he had not been physically aggressive, people felt it was simply a matter of time. In general, he would storm out of a classroom and find an empty room in which to rage. On a few occasions, he bolted from the school building but remained on the playground. In spite of these difficulties, it became evident on further exploration that his temper was not consistently hair-trigger. More accurately, there were signs that his anxiety was building, and if heeded, he could turn things around and maintain himself in class. When these signs were not addressed, however, he indeed became edgy to the point where the smallest issues could lead to an explosion.

Some of Todd's teachers seemed to intuitively understand his anxiety and could find ways on their own to redirect him before he became agitated. Other teachers did not anticipate as well, and language arts was often—but not always—a challenge for him due to his discomfort over his learning disability. In these situations, there were times when Todd would lose self-control. Yet there was no single precipitating event, no predictable precursor that one could clearly identify. Something that would set him off one day would be inconsequential the next. But, as noted, there were various signs reflecting a buildup of his anxiety: his legs would bounce up and down. He grinded his teeth; took on a serious, almost menacing look; and muttered to himself. All these signs were readily observable to me since I had the luxury of doing nothing else in the class but watch him. At times he snapped pencils, but generally, he was already past his ability to cope when this occurred.

The focus shifted from responding to blowups to establishing ways to prevent them. Initially, the team came together to develop a common language for letting Todd know that he was showing signs of a buildup in his anxiety. Much to members' surprise, Todd was intrigued by this process since he felt distressed by his out-of-control behavior and had demonstrated little prior awareness that events might be heading in such a direction. He was able to articulate how little he liked feeling or acting in such a way, especially because—as a 13-year-old—he worried about the perceptions of his peers. He was equally fascinated by the idea of anxiety as a process of surging-up; we used the metaphor of "steam in the pot" to help him make sense of this. Todd's capacity to cope increased with the addition of a few simple strategies based on a different way of understanding his behavior; that is, as the result of an accumulation of stressors, rather than as a specific set of events (or a bad attitude). As an additional note, another helping step was the school's willingness to provide him with resource room language arts as his full inclusion was simply too much for him to handle. And on the less frequent occasions in which he did blow up, there was a predetermined quiet place for him to go within the building, and he readily headed there when needed.

Earl, a 13-year-old with high-functioning autism, is both intelligent and verbal. He performs well in school, especially in a resource room setting that has fewer students and more adults to guide the classroom. Although historically, he has never been viewed as a student with problematic behavior, there have been recent signs of this, including head-banging (against a desk), masturbating, and running out of the classroom. My theory in this case is that Earl was being pushed too hard in school due to his strong skills and his history, if you will, of nonprotest. He has always done what was asked of him. The interventions were based on such a premise. As a middle school student, the academic demands build over the course of a year, and it was simply too challenging for Earl to keep up the pace, even though he understood the concepts and could, with great effort, sustain his level of performance. A useful metaphor, which I shared with his team, is that of a runner's sprint. One can move at high speed for a period of time, but there is no one who can maintain such a peak. My sense of Earl's school experience—which he could not or would not articulate for himself—was that the academic expectations were based on his highest, rather than his average, speed. He was being pushed far beyond what he could sustain. The recommended interventions were well received by his team, which built in daily break times, reduced his homework, and allowed him to do a reduced amount of writing (an act that fatigued him). He also spent less of his day transitioning in and out of regular classrooms. It took a while, but there was gradual progress in Earl's behavior. The act of renewal is not an immediate one, just as the accumulation of anxiety takes time to build, but there was a clear trend toward less anxious behavior.

RECOGNIZE THAT SOME CHILDREN HAVE A REDUCED THRESHOLD OF TOLERANCE FOR FRUSTRATION

Like the idea that there can be an accumulation of anxiety that underlies a breakdown in behavior, some children have a lowered threshold of frustration tolerance that, when crossed, will lead to disruptive behavior. The example of Todd (discussed previously) can also be construed in this way; that is, the goal of helping him manage the buildup of anxiety parallels the notion that some children, especially those with less capacity to manage their attention, stimulation level, mood, and/or behavior, will melt down once they have gone over their threshold. This includes children with ADHD and coexisting behavioral disorders as well as those with brain injuries, psychotic disorders, bipolar disorder, and trauma. It also includes children without any formal mental health diagnosis who seem constitutionally unable to handle much in the way of frustration.

Threshold is the precise word I use with children as well as with their teachers and parents because it provides a visual picture that clarifies the concept. While it is an invisible line in the sand, adults usually can identify that a child has arrived at such a point, which often leads to a manage-the-crisis mode. The objective is to use preventive strategies so that a child does not cross that threshold. Knowing the nuances of a particular child, recognizing when he is getting close to a trouble point, and, ultimately, maintaining the kind of relationship that allows for that recognition to emerge are central components.

To illustrate such an idea, the following is the case of Keith. A fifth grader in a rural town, he has been diagnosed with many disorders, and these often change according to the clinical judgment of the particular clinical evaluator. My impression is that he does not fit comfortably into any particular category but clearly has a threshold issue. Teachers and parents note his behavioral outbursts, which have become less aggressive over time but remain volatile—and they have an impact on his social relations. His parents were surprised when one of my questions was whether he takes long and unusually hot showers—they answered yes. In my mind, his sensory issues were a significant part of his struggle, along with his inability to manage his mood and, ultimately, his behavior. Keith takes these lengthy showers after a bad day at school as a way for him to keep things in check at home. Every strategy we put into place at school, including a quiet lunch with a peer, a special recess (with, at most, three other children), sensory breaks during the morning and afternoon, and a resource room period in which he could work independently, served as an attempt to avoid his crossing his threshold.

BE AWARE THAT SOME CHILDREN ARE CONSTITUTIONALLY UNABLE TO "GO WITH THE FLOW" OR HANDLE CHANGES TO THEIR REGULAR ROUTINES

Similar to the previous notion that some children have a reduced tolerance for frustration is the related idea that there are children who are rigid and inflexible. This can be due to genetics, temperament, an unsafe living environment, or a combination of all these factors. Parents and teachers often struggle with how to help such children because, as we know, life generally does not work according to plan. A regular school day may entail a change in teachers if someone is out sick. There may be an assembly, a fire drill, a "special" class, a half-day due to professional development for teachers or conferences with parents—there are a host of reasons why a particular school day may not fit with the child's expectations. I find that there is general acceptance of this notion for children with autistic spectrum disorders but often a much lower level of acknowledgment—or even belief that this might exist—for other children.

Yet children with trauma histories are often agitated by unanticipated changes to their day, especially if these involve an adjustment in which they will need to interact. Since, as noted in the discussion of PTSD, an aura of safety and predictability underlies the capacity for many children to maintain their attention, mood, and behavior, even small changes can lead to significant behavioral flare-ups. Similarly, children with ADHD may struggle to make sense of the flow of their day and become anxious and distracted by unexpected alterations to the schedule. What helps is to teach children how to anticipate, problem solve, and even appreciate change. This is a much bigger task for some children in comparison to others, and a judgment needs to be made concerning a specific child's capacity in this area. Some need to be forewarned about impending fire drills (and the sound of the alarm) and any other known changes in schedule. Rarely is there a concerted attempt to teach children how to manage change, yet it is an intervention that can go a long way toward helping them with this ongoing reality of life. Moreover, it is valuable to remember that we—the adults—need to be equally if not more flexible so as to assist children with this same task.

Gerry, an 11-year-old diagnosed with trauma, ADHD, and OCD, is a prime example of the inability to tolerate change. For him, any alteration to his physical space, schedule, or regular teaching staff is enough either to bring him to tears or, more frequently, cause an eruption. The latter results in yelling, cursing, and the need to remove him from class as quickly as possible. The observation, therefore, that he scares his classmates should not be surprising. Because he is an exceptionally bright child, adults were long suspicious that these behaviors were intentional or, at least, within his control. It was only when the school psychologist did an FBA that the pattern to this behavior became apparent. The intervention, which was led by this same psychologist and grounded in cognitive behavioral principles, was to help Gerry put a grade to the various changes he might need to face in school; that is, he rated the degree of difficulty involved in trying to cope with these adjustments to his day. Some he was quickly able to figure out strategies for maintaining himself, others required specific comments or help from the adults around him, and a few remaining ones remained stressful enough that he needed to bolt to a safe place just outside the classroom. It took four half-hour meetings to achieve this. Overall, these steps represented major progress for him, and it certainly helped in terms of his peer relationships. It was also an eye-opening experience for school staff as they needed to revamp their long-held view of Gerry's behavior and make sense of his apparent resistance to change.

Notably, not every child who is inflexible carries a formal diagnosis. All of us are on a continuum with this, from highly flexible to rigid, and most of us are better in some situations than others and at particular times. I know children who are generally able to tolerate changes at home but cannot do this in school—and vice versa. These observations reflect the individualized nature of children's behaviors and reinforce the idea that context matters when trying to understand their meaning.

TEACH CHILDREN SELF-CALMING STRATEGIES

In accordance with the high rates of children with anxiety—and whether or not their anxiety reaches the threshold for a specific diagnosis—teaching children early on about ways to cope with anxiety is an important strategy. One might argue that this is a parent function, but schools bring different forms of stress to children and are uniquely positioned to address them. Given the move toward high-stakes testing in schools, this becomes an even more significant concern. School settings offer health education (which usually includes a segment about sexuality) and teach other kinds of personal and social development topics, so incorporating a component on managing anxiety is not an implausible notion. Moreover, this does not require a substantial commitment of time. Providing children with basic information about stress and interventions such as visual imagery, diaphragmatic breathing, and progressive muscle relaxation would allow them to practice these skills in the actual setting in which they may need to utilize them. One elementary school has its students practice relaxation every morning for less than five minutes, and the principal reports that this single strategy has helped a vast number of students over the years. He notes that, as a class-wide intervention, it removes the stigma and embarrassment from more anxious students who desperately need to be rehearsing and enacting such skills.

Occupational therapists are often additional resources in developing these interventions, given their expertise in understanding children with sensory needs—that is, the struggle to manage one's level of stimulation and, consequently, sense of calm. Some schools—and parents as well—have adapted the principles of yoga as a method for teaching relaxation to children. I have observed schools that instituted yoga as part of their daily routine and have also seen—on occasion—physical education teachers use this as part of their curriculum.

DELINEATE WHEN AN ADULT WILL BE RETURNING

This is especially helpful for anxious children, children with PTSD, those with traumatic brain injuries (TBIs), or anyone who has difficulty holding ideas in his head (deficits in working memory, often seen in children with ADHD). To use current neuropsychological language, one refers to children with deficits in executive functioning. These are the same kids that are often reported to be blurting out when they get an idea. Kids with a poor sense of the passage of time (e.g., kids with ADHD) often benefit from assistance in this way, or otherwise, they may attempt to keep an adult attuned to them at all times; that is, they may not be able to tolerate the person's departure because they will not know how to predict when he or she will return. In so many of these instances, the child's behavior is perceived as attention seeking or oppositional, but I have found that this one simple technique reduces a number of such overt concerns, notably in school settings.

DO NOT OVERSTRESS PERFECTION

Good enough behavior should be the goal, not the avoidance of all errors. Psychoanalytic theorist and practitioner D. W. Winnicott coined the notion of "good enough" in the literature on psychodynamic therapy, suggesting that aiming for a reasonable level of goodness is healthier and, ultimately, more productive. While the concept was developed within a framework for exploring mother-child interactions, we generally seem to accept this idea in the context of adult behavior, but there is often surprisingly little margin for error granted to children. Frequently, for example, behavior plans are created that give bonuses for so-called perfect behavior, yet I find these plans to be counterproductive. They suggest to children that one should strive for an unsustainable level of performance and imply that anything less is substandard. This conception is magnified for children who present with (or have underlying) anxiety and/or depression as well as specific behavioral concerns.

For example, I observed an interaction between a teacher and student in which the teacher announced that the child had earned his reward for the afternoon but had "done better" the previous day. When this 10-year-old boy looked confused, she told him that he had earned all of his stars yesterday but not today. The conveyed message, of course, was that his current success was not all that meaningful. In this behavioral classroom, there was a special reward for students who had perfect days of behavior. Given that this boy had a lengthy history of social failure and peer rejection and was now not much of a risk taker (academically or socially), such a scenario reinforced the idea that he should quietly hang back and avoid interacting with his peers since this was the domain that typically led to his loss of stars. To me, a child in a behavioral class who has a *good* day, with some normal ups and downs, is on a better track than one who has a perfect day because the latter is impossible to maintain. It is the capacity to bounce back from life's inevitable disappointments and failures, to turn oneself around after a poor choice, that signifies real progress. Yet the message this boy took away with him was that he had performed better the day before when he achieved an arbitrary measure of flawlessness. The way for children to develop resilience is to hold the belief that they can overcome their mistakes and still be successful, rather than internalize the idea that they must avoid all errors in living. The latter is an unfair and even imposing assumption, yet we condition children in exactly such a way when we emphasize perfection. Behavioral interventions should be constructed to account for the need for good enough behavior.

AVOID USING NEEDED INTERVENTIONS AS REWARDS

It is more effective—and humane—to avoid using breaks or sensory inputs as rewards when kids need these to cope. While this idea may seem obvious, its merits are often overlooked in the rush to control children's behavior. On one occasion, I consulted on a case in which a child with clear sensory dysfunction (he became overstimulated by both loud noises and bright fluorescent lighting) was denied time in an occupational therapy room where he could get the sensory inputs he required to remain calm. As these breaks were further denied, his behavior deteriorated. It was not until these sensory breaks were consistently built back into his schedule and were no longer contingent on specific behavior that he began to calm down.

RECOGNIZE THE ALTERNATIVE LEARNING CURVE—AND NEEDS—OF CHILDREN WITH LEARNING AND DEVELOPMENTAL DISABILITIES

While other writers and researchers (Mel Levine, for example) have alluded to this idea, it often gets ignored in practice, especially when schools are confronted with a child whose behavior is disagreeable and distracting. For children with AS, for example, it is not unusual to see a long period of what is known as *consolidation*. This is the time where children take in, make sense of, and integrate what they have learned. In my experience, children with AS often have far longer periods of consolidation than other children, intermittent with sudden bursts of new learning and growth. Similarly, children with specific learning needs may plateau at particular points in the curriculum and require modified approaches to help them grasp the material. Teachers, parents, and children need to be aware of patterns such as this to reduce everyone's level of frustration. Too often, I hear about children who "lack motivation," without a firm understanding of their cognitive and academic development. It is the resultant loss of confidence and task persistence that becomes the bigger problem and contributes to either acting-out or shutting-down behavior.

A prototype of this kind of scenario concerns Terrance, a 12-year-old with learning disabilities in reading and, to a lesser extent, math. Terrance is bright, friendly, popular—and task-avoidant during almost any task that involves reading. He is acutely self-aware of his learning issues and makes jokes, interrupts, and takes frequent trips to the bathroom, especially during classes where he might be called on to read aloud. It was not difficult to make sense of Terrance's behavior, nor was he particularly reticent to admit to what was happening when he was finally asked directly. He articulated that it was better, from a social standpoint, to be seen as a cutup than as stupid. This is not an unusual perception for children with learning disabilities, especially at his age, and schools need to work with such children to help them understand the nature of their learning issues. In Terrance's case, it was a simple set of strategies that gradually turned things around; classroom teachers no longer asked any of the children to read aloud (or, if so, they requested volunteers), his in-class assignments were more carefully modified to meet his actual performance level, and Terrance held two meetings with the school counselor to gather information about learning disabilities. As school counselors often observe when undertaking this process, many children are shocked to learn that famous and accomplished people have had learning disabilities of one form or another. For Terrance, it helped to take the pressure off and, in general, left him less vigilant about how others might perceive him. While some of the adjustment needed to come from Terrance, the school played a significant role in helping him feel more comfortable and, ultimately, willing to take risks with his schoolwork.

FOR CHILDREN WITH LEARNING DISABILITIES OR GLOBAL LEARNING PROBLEMS, RECOGNIZE THAT TASK MASTERY IS TYPICALLY MORE IMPORTANT THAN INDEPENDENCE

At times, adults' priorities differ dramatically from those of children. One of the primary complaints raised in schools, especially during the middle school years, concerns children who demand constant attention and appear unwilling to work without assistance. One way of understanding this common phenomenon is that children are enticed more by performing a task successfully than by doing it themselves. Adults tend to focus more on the latter, mindful of the importance of independent work and the growing significance of this as children progress through school. Yet anxious children may demand an adult's presence to take any kind of academic risk, and a potential stalemate is enacted. One way around this is to name the pattern and, as noted earlier, to identify when the adult will return. I have told children that I will come back when they have, initially, tried one problem on their own. The frequency can then be gradually weaned back. The fear that this will take too much time is, in my mind, unfounded, in that the adult is probably already devoting an inordinate amount of time to this child anyway. From a developmental perspective, I have found that independence follows mastery, and that greater emphasis on the latter will inevitably lead to more of the former.

An example concerns Maria, a seventh grader with a language-based learning disability and an anxious style who began to shut down in school. Her parent was alarmed. Maria had little to say about it other than that she hated school. Discussions with her school staff revealed that, philosophically, they held independent work in the highest regard and expected students to learn how to function without constant teacher input. Their belief, in essence, was that children were spoon-fed prior to their arrival in seventh grade. While it appeared to be a useful strategy for many of the students to work more independently, it was disastrous for Maria. She was unwilling to take risks with her academic work and gave up when she perceived the adults pulling away from her. While this remains a work in progress, the school has started to recognize that Maria's pattern is to do more on her own when she feels confident in her ability to handle the content. As such, the teachers have begun to provide support based on this understanding.

LIMIT THE USE OF TIME-OUT

Whole books could be devoted to the use and misuse of time-out procedures, but there are a couple of critical ideas to keep in mind. Most important, only use time-out with children who have the ability to calm themselves. Many children who are hyperactive, anxious, or, for that matter, explosive cannot soothe themselves when things have become escalated. Paradoxically, the time-out exacerbates their prevailing affective state, leading to a worsening of the behavior. At times, children who have managed to maintain their cool will blow up as a result of being sent to time-out. More helpful is the use of a quiet space where an adult may quietly sit with the child. Time-out, which must be tied to the developmental age of the child, should only be utilized after other approaches have failed, not as an initial response to behavior. Traditionally, the recommendation has been one minute per year of age; that is, a five-year-old should be given a five-minute time-out. The only problem is that some five-year-olds cannot begin to tolerate sitting that long, especially alone, which reminds us that any judgment about the appropriate length of time needs to be based on an understanding of the individual child. There are instances, frankly, in which a time-out is employed because the adult lacks other available tools; the child does not necessarily require this to hold himself together. From this perspective, overuse is not merely an unsuccessful strategy; it can lead to a consistently resentful child.

OFFER REPLACEMENT OPTIONS

These are also known as *substitution behaviors*. Impulsive children often get themselves into trouble for something they say without thinking about it first. There probably is not a single teacher who has not had a student like this. In some instances, it makes sense to simply give a consequence to the child if, for example, the comments were hurtful to others. In other situations, though, it might make more sense to provide the child with a possible out; that is, one might ask the child to say it in another way first. I have had numerous children who, when given a second opportunity (even if the motivation is simply to avoid a consequence), will grab onto it. This strategy also opens up a teachable moment if the child is not sure just how else to put it. To repeat: any strategy should be based on a presumption about the meaning of the behavior. Only those situations in which one concludes that what was said deserves a chance to be restated should invoke this technique. Similarly, for younger children, the opportunity to do it another way should be considered. Not every behavior or utterance needs to have a consequence, and often, it is the skill of the adult involved in a situation that determines the effectiveness of the outcome.

USE VISUAL CUES

Culturally, we do not seem to understand how useful this can be for children, even if, as adults, some of us live out of our appointment books. Many adults feel that the act of writing things down helps them to remember these events—this is an internalizing of what was made visual. So why deny children the same forms of support? Hodgdon (1995) and, later, Gray (2000) supplied strong arguments in favor of employing visual supports, based on the literature concerning children with autistic spectrum disorders.[52,53] Such children become overwhelmed by spoken language and perform best when instructions can be referenced visually, yet there is often much resistance to providing such support. Similarly, children with ADHD are notoriously described as "not listening," yet many are efficient users of visual and tactile cues. As such, it is worthwhile to experiment with using these, especially for children who experience difficulty in making sense of spoken language. Anxious behavior is often misinterpreted as oppositional behavior (which may, in fact, be exactly what it feels like to a busy teacher or parent), and visual cuing is one way to investigate whether a particular behavior belongs more in the former or latter category.

CHOOSE THE PROPER TIME TO PROCESS WITH THE CHILD CONCERNING HIS BEHAVIOR

For children who are angry or even explosive, there is little to be gained by pushing them to be insightful about their behavior while they remain agitated. Yet this is frequently what occurs. I have witnessed small incidents become much larger ones because, as adults, we push children to take ownership of what transpired or at least make sense of their own part in it. At times, the expressed fear is that the child may not connect the behavior to an outcome if time elapses, and sometimes the issue is that we simply do not want children to perceive that they got away with something. Conversely, these goals are least likely to be met if the child is too angry to process the issues of meaning and responsibility in the moment. Allowing time for the child to cool off is inherently more practical and effective and, in addition, models our own capacity to manage strong emotions. There is no substitute for knowing the child and his general capacities in this area—and sometimes I simply ask if he is ready. Employing such an approach evokes no loss of authority.

FLOAT IDEAS ABOUT THE MEANING OF THE CHILD'S BEHAVIOR RATHER THAN DEMANDING ACKNOWLEDGMENT

This notion, a corollary to the previous one, is useful in getting defensive or angry children to address their own behavior. Insistence on gaining a specific admission from the child may lead to further confrontation, whereas a more speculative method may elicit greater cooperation and openness. In the case of two eight-year-old boys where one hit the other, for example, using the statement "I wonder if you hit John because you were angry he took your pencil" is more likely to be effective than starting with "Why did you do that? Tell me why you hit John." In this scenario, as in many like it, an initial emphasis on the affect rather than the resultant behavior opens up to a discussion of the behavior itself. In my experience, one only stirs up more resistance if the discussion begins with an accusation or interrogation. Attempting to walk around the resistance is not about backing down from unacceptable behavior; rather, it is a more practical strategy for confronting it directly and facilitating learning.

AVOID APPROACHES TO PUNISHMENT THAT CONSIST PRIMARILY OF TAKING AWAY FROM CHILDREN

While an approach like this may be helpful in some situations, it is most clearly not beneficial when dealing with angry, depressed children. One of the questions I am asked most frequently by schools and parents is why their children's conduct does not improve when they are told they will forfeit various objects or privileges if particular behaviors continue. In fact, many of these adults observe that, paradoxically, the behavior worsens. My response is that taking away from children who, in the vernacular, would rather die than give in only increases their level of depression, alienation, and distress. In many instances, children simply blow up. It is not unusual, for example, for schools (or parents) to take away after-school activities when a child is performing poorly in school. Depressed children, though, tend to become more hopeless because this results in even less to look forward to. Since the idea of instituting a punishment is linked to the goal of a better outcome, this obviously is not effective. Instead, many of these children need ways to reengage with adults or the larger school culture; that is, we need to assist them in the process of seeking meaningful connections, a complex practice when trying to help an aggrieved child hook up with what may be an equally resentful environment. For many children, depending on their makeup and the nature of their behavior, interventions that are positive and incentive-driven are more likely to be successful contributors to the process.

PROVIDE REGULAR CHECK-IN TIMES FOR CHILDREN WHO ARE DEPRESSED, ANXIOUS, OR TRAUMATIZED

This strategy has been highly beneficial in a number of situations. While school administrators generally do not like to think of their settings as therapeutic, this is a very simple and direct service that can reflect the difference between success and failure for particular children. An example follows: a high school where I consult asked for help with a teenage girl who had been sexually assaulted and was just now returning to school. She reported high anxiety about leaving home and reengaging in her life prior to the traumatizing event (which did not take place at school). We arranged for her to hold three meetings per day, each five minutes long, with different adults in the high school. The containment and sense of safety this provided her, and the resultant decrease in anxiety, was valuable in helping to improve her functioning, both academic and social. After a few weeks, we weaned this back to two meetings per day, and then one. While we left open this single meeting, she rarely used it, though she reported that knowing it was there made her feel better. This time was not therapy. She met in the morning with a teacher who simply talked about the expectations for the day, helped her to review her schedule, and created a sense of safety. Only one of the three meetings was scheduled with a counselor, and again, the time was utilized to calm and focus her. The initial commitment of 15 minutes per day was minimal by any standard, yet it offered her a way back into school. I have used this approach in many cases with a range of present-ing clinical issues, generally with great success. Often, it is those chil-dren with anxiety and/or trauma who benefit most noticeably.

OFFER ORGANIZATIONAL CHECK-IN TIME
FOR CHILDREN WITH ATTENTION-DEFICIT/
HYPERACTIVITY DISORDER AND OTHERS
WHO NEED THIS

This strategy is a corollary to the previous one, though it emphasizes different skills and different presenting issues. One of the primary com-plaints by teachers is the lack of students' organizational skills—and such complaints appear to be on the rise. Given this, schools can offer a brief period each day where children receive direct help in organizing homework, long-term assignments, and materials. The work does not need to be done *for* children; rather, they should receive the support and structure to develop these skills themselves. Just as schools provide study periods for children to rehearse and integrate academic content, they can similarly allot time to address organizational tasks. By defini-tion, people with ADHD have difficulty in organizing themselves, so it seems a reasonable and advantageous accommodation to emphasize (and teach) the necessary skills. It is a minimal commitment of time that can have a huge payback for everyone involved. I have seen this success-fully accomplished in less than 15 minutes per day. In some instances, it makes sense to offer an initial check-in at the beginning of the morning to prepare for the day. At the end of the day, the time can be utilized to review homework and prepare for the transition out of the school setting.

APPLY A DEVELOPMENTAL PERSPECTIVE TO
MAKING SENSE OF A CHILD'S BEHAVIOR

Like many strategic interventions, this sounds somewhat obvious. Yet it is a frequent occurrence that such a perspective is lost when a child's behavior becomes intolerable to a teacher or parent. A recent example involves a family with a precocious four-year-old who came in to see me last year, with the parents understandably exasperated by the child's challenging behavior. What we eventually concluded was that this little boy had figured out, on a cognitive level, that he could control his parents. He was stimulated by mastering the particular skill of interper-sonal cause and effect. His intellectual capacity allowed him to master a task that his emotional level of development could not begin to understand or approximate. He was not immune to his parents' upset but could not fully grasp his place in it. Finally, with some strained patience on the parents' part and recognition that this was not necessarily planned behavior on the boy's part, the family settled into a less overwrought pattern. Fortunately, at least according to the parents' later reports, this child's emotional development began to catch up with his cognitive skill, and the behavior evolved into less contentious forms. A similar developmental perspective toward children's behavior, from early childhood through adolescence, can be helpful in reducing the sense that the child is out to get the adults in his life.

Another example of developmental thinking pertains to a recent case of a first-grade boy. He was diagnosed with ADHD and was often described as defiant, oppositional, or difficult. Yet, on a review of his history and a short period of observation, it was evident that he functioned like a preschooler in almost every area of development, whether academic, social, or behavioral. The idea that he should be expected to "act his age" made no sense because he was incapable of doing so. No prodding or threats could alter this scenario, much to the chagrin of those who worked directly with him. The intervention that turned things around was simple, if not mildly controversial among school administrators: he was returned to a kindergarten classroom. His behavior improved markedly, and he no longer presented in school as though he had ADHD as his performance matched that of the younger cohort. His capacity to wait, for example, was now consistent with that displayed by his classmates. While this sounds like a simple formulation, it was not an easy or linear process. The need to recognize and respond sensitively to children's uneven developmental growth is paramount to improving their overall performance. Such considerations should continue throughout childhood, not solely with regard to younger children.

TEACH CHILDREN ABOUT LIMIT SETTING

A strategy I have found useful in numerous situations is to explore with children their understanding of limits, how these translate into what teachers and parents say, and, ultimately, how to anticipate the ways in which people will respond in particular situations. Perhaps this is simply a variant of what has come to be known as emotional intelligence (see Goleman, 1995), in which an emphasis is placed on, among other things, the development of social "astuteness."[54] This kind of teaching can be very helpful for children with behavioral disorders, who are often unable to employ such anticipatory skills—or simply lack the experience in attempting it. A question I have posed to many children labeled as "acting out" is, What happens when you do that? How will your teacher (parent, principal) respond to that sort of thing? What will the consequence to you look like? It may sound as though these are obvious questions, but in my experience, they are often posed when the child is already in trouble, rather than at a time when the child may be able to utilize the concepts in a teachable, preventive way.

RESPOND EFFECTIVELY TO THE "HE ALWAYS NEEDS TO HAVE THE LAST WORD" CHALLENGE

This concern is especially prevalent among teenagers, though it can occur at any age. There are two simple strategies for coping with it, and the choice comes down to personal style and the larger context in which the problem is occurring. One is simply to name that the other person typically wants the last word and, as such, should have it. No argument ensues, and much of the potency in having the final say disappears. Some children stare at me in disbelief when I make such an offer because they are habituated to the idea that they need to stake out their ground to achieve what they consider a position of control. I find that an offer of the final say is the most common way for me to handle such a scenario. Another is to set a limit by again naming it but, in this case, stating that the adult will have the final say on the matter at hand and that any attempt to have the last word will lead to a consequence. While there are times (and children) in which such a deterrent strategy might make sense, the first option serves as a form of redirection and reduces friction. It transcends the battle over what is usually—in reality—an unimportant component of the dynamic in the moment. It helps to keep the focus on the larger issues.

The following two strategies, while strategic and practice based, are rooted in a larger discussion about social skills development and the notion of emotional intelligence. According to Salovey and Grewal (2005), emotional intelligence is critical to both personal and work relationships.[55] While this seems on the surface to be an obvious finding, little in the way of hard research has been conducted up to now to validate such an idea. The authors point to "accumulating evidence" concerning the significance of this form of intelligence. They detail a four-prong model: (1) perceiving emotions, which entails the capacity to identify others' and one's own emotions; (2) understanding emotions, which relates to recognizing "slight variations between emotions," such as the distinction between happy and ecstatic; (3) using emotions, the ability to "make effective use" of how one feels in order to problem solve situations; and (4) managing emotions, the notion of managing oneself as well as the strong feelings of others. I mention this model in particular because it demonstrates the importance of emotional intelligence throughout the life span and therefore gives rise to the issue of children's need for good modeling from adults. While it supports one of the primary ideas in this book, that relationships are crucial to children's healthy development, it also gives credence for providing concrete feedback to children that teaches them about their behavior and its impact on others as well as themselves.

ASSIST CHILDREN WITH SOCIAL SKILLS DEFICITS AS TO THEIR PRAGMATIC SKILLS, INCLUDING THEIR INITIATION (OR ENTRY) STRATEGIES

Many children, notably those with AS or nonverbal learning disabilities, but also those with ADHD, have difficulty in starting conversations or figuring out ways to successfully navigate the process of interacting in groups. There is an emerging literature concerning the broad issue of social skills development, though McGinnis, Goldstein, Sprafkin, and Gershaw (1984) were early proponents of intervening from a teaching perspective.[56] An increasing number of schools are offering social skills groups, which signifies that there is a growing recognition of the issue. A primary concern for children is often what to say or do at the outset of an interaction, and the skills necessary for this can be taught, rehearsed, and maintained. It is often a labor-intensive process to both learn and teach social skills, especially when they are not understood on an intuitive level. (People with AS, for example, may appear somewhat awkward and rigid, even when they know *what* to say during such situations.) Nonetheless, teaching specific skills that children need to survive socially in schools is a worthy endeavor. The work of McAfee (2002) as well as other researchers in the autism field has shed greater light on this area.[57]

An extension of this idea is to teach children how to recognize when the social strategies they employ are unsuccessful. During observations of elementary school children in the lunchroom or at recess, it is usually easy to pick out those who are having social difficulties, as these challenges are most apparent during less structured times of the school day. Hall passing and the daily bus ride are also times in which such difficulties routinely emerge. One of the notable findings is that children who struggle socially tend to have a limited repertoire of interactional skills available to them; that is, they often try the same approaches over and over rather than altering them to fit the situation. Trying harder with the same set of strategies typically leads to repeated failure and often results in frustration and even rage on the part of the child who is unsuccessful. One method for helping children is to recognize and address these patterns in small-group skills groups. It is especially useful if the group leader can independently observe children's interactions to identify what the child may not be able to self-report. Many emotional and behavioral problems manifested in school settings, whether internal in nature, such as anxiety (e.g., school avoidance), or externalized via acting-out behavior, can be linked to such interpersonal struggles.

TEACH CHILDREN HOW TO IDENTIFY PROBLEMS AND HOW TO SOLVE THEM

An extension of the prior principle is that children with social skills deficits, including those with AS as well as some with varying degrees of ADHD, trauma, high anxiety, and depression, often have difficulty recognizing and interpreting problematic interactions. Many social skills curricula and on-site programs I have observed focus on how to solve problems but assume that children understand the context that led to the problem. If a social scenario was misunderstood, it simply makes no sense to apply problem-solving strategies to it. Emphasizing recognition, becoming aware that one may have mistaken the words or intent of another child, developing ways to check out one's understanding—each of these contributes to fewer social problems and, subsequently, leaves room for implementing specific problem-solving strategies. This idea augments rather than replaces the kinds of social skills teaching often found in schools.

An example of this principle follows: Billy, a nine-year-old with both anxiety and severe ADHD, presented as a boy in perpetual motion. Teachers referred to him as a "whirlwind," a title also used at home by his parents. One notable aspect of this case is that, while his parents were forthcoming about Billy's diagnoses, they were clear that medication was not under consideration. Other third graders seemed to like his cheerful disposition but were generally confused by his behavior, especially during recess and other less structured times. He spoke and moved rapidly and, equally, was unpredictable in terms of their expectations of how nine-year-olds should act. During recess he would sometimes join games in which he had not been involved, or disappear suddenly from a team in which he had been a member. This was clearly disconcerting to the other children, and confrontations would occasionally ensue. Billy moved through events so chaotically that he truly had no idea what the fuss was about, so any attempt to get him to solve the problem (with questions like "What could you have done instead, Billy?") went nowhere. While Billy learned to mouth some version of the correct words that resembled a solution, one look at his face revealed that he was totally perplexed. More to the point, his behavior did not change. Eventually, the school's approach shifted to one of helping him recognize what the problem was and how other children understood it. When he had difficulty on the playground, the monitor would name what was happening in language that had been previously discussed so that Billy could make sense of what he was being told. He was also given reminders before going outside. This helped him to a degree, but certainly not fully. Subsequently, the school instituted just one solution that was, in fact, suggested by Billy: he wanted to run a lap around the track every time he heard his reminder. In many ways, this was his rather creative attempt to generate his own solution, by pulling himself away from other kids before he became embroiled in a confrontation. Over time, he learned to divert himself without prompting from adults, which implies that his capacity to recognize the problem had improved, but he continued to need a separate activity to be successful. It would not be surprising, based on his presentation, that individual pursuits might continue to be a more viable option for him during at least a portion of unstructured activities.

PROMPT CHILDREN WITH QUESTIONS
RATHER THAN DEMANDS

Many children—and not just teenagers—report during therapy that they simply shut down in terms of what adults tell them to do. There is often a sense that they hear what they are told but are not necessarily listening. Or, conversely, they simply respond to demands by rote obedience. ("I do it so the teacher will get off my case," states one 10-year-old girl.) As many parents, teachers, and counselors know, some children simply nod in agreement to whatever it is that adults say, with little to no follow-through. A valuable strategy is to prompt children by asking them what needs to be done rather than telling them. For example, it is often helpful to ask a child "What am I going to say?" or "What do you think is likely to happen right now?" While this sounds like a simple intervention, it frequently gets lost in the rush to maintain a busy classroom or family at home. Responding to a question necessitates processing the request and developing a response and often leads to both better behavior and a more thoughtful child. Self-generated strategies reveal the problem-solving capacities of children and give them greater ownership of the solution.

ADDRESS ENVIRONMENTAL OR CULTURAL ISSUES THAT IMPACT CHILDREN IN SCHOOLS

Saphier and Gower (1997; the first edition was published in 1979) employed the word *culture* to explore the fit between children and their larger environments.[58] Similarly, Garbarino's (1995) classic work focused on the ways in which underprivileged, unsupported environments contribute to a child's poor performance.[59] These authors, in different ways, opened the door to looking at how such ingrained factors as race, socioeconomic status, and gender (which are of themselves difficult and unpopular conversations within many settings) may intersect with observed behavior. I have met with children who, due to any or all of these factors, reported feeling that they do not belong. In some instances, it was overt behavior that communicated such a message prior to these children attaching any language to their experience. While this is, to a degree, a typical developmental occurrence for many adolescents, it is magnified in those for whom there are very real differences. Fitting in is especially salient during the middle school years, and such negatively felt experiences may emerge in critical ways during that time. Clearly school communities need to be responsive to these concerns. Allowing children the opportunity to explore and gain a greater understanding of personal differences—in an ongoing manner—can be helpful in reducing isolation and mistrust. It also helps to ask directly children who are struggling behaviorally about their perception of and experience with these factors.

Furthermore, school communities need to be sensitive to the content of children's outside lives. Kozol (1991, 1995, 2005), throughout his body of work, reminds us in stark terms of how challenging day-to-day life is for far too many children.[60-62] The context of poverty, absent or struggling parents, racism and other forms of discrimination, bullying, traumatic environments, lack of social supports, and/or other similar factors are embedded in how the child defines himself and what his behavior may represent; the argument here is not for simplifying our understanding of children's complex lives, but rather integrating such factors into our consideration of ways to support them. Nonetheless, there are limits to what schools can provide, as many districts report that they are being asked to pay for and deliver services that have traditionally been offered by other governmental agencies. The basis for the approaches offered in this book is that schools should focus on success in school; that is, we should strive to provide an affirming experience in spite of very real and pressing outside concerns and confront external obstacles as best we can. Most children quickly grasp the notion that what is expected of them in school is different than how they may act in other settings, whether they follow through on these expectations or not. Emphasizing here-and-now success is a way to help children begin the process of learning how to compartmentalize their lives, such that they expand their awareness that school can be a safe and sustaining environment, even if other settings are not. It is less helpful to bemoan the external factors that schools cannot control or sometimes even impact in the slightest.

TEACH CHILDREN NOT TO GIVE IN TO DESPAIR

This simple statement is rooted in a complex notion. Hopelessness is a hallmark of depression and, as a discrete factor, is more highly correlated with suicide than is level of depression (Beck, 1999).[63] Therefore the effort to combat hopelessness in children is more than a lofty ideal. One way to cultivate a sense of hope and self-agency among children is to implement practices that reflect optimism and the belief that children can succeed. I have seen the same behavioral model used in disparate ways, both to nurture and support children, but also, unfortunately, as a sort of weapon to indicate a child's failings. As caregivers, we make the choice as to how we will implement the strategies available to us. If nothing else, a child with, for example, OCD or, conversely, a history of rageful behavior needs to know that someone believes he can improve. Struggling children can be anchored by such a positive attitude. Another way to foster hope among children is to ensure that caregivers, including school staff, are equally resilient and optimistic about the future. This can be a challenging task for teachers, counselors, and parents, especially given the complexity of the children we serve and the stressed environments in which many of us function. Nonetheless, adults must model hope for children, and as noted above, it helps to focus on what we can achieve rather than what is unattainable. The translation of this comment is not that we should accept inferior conditions or unjust practices, but rather that we attempt to work meaningfully, purposefully, and collaboratively toward altering them. As one adolescent told me, children scrutinize adults' behavior all the time, whether we are aware of it or not.

Not all noncompliant behaviors are meant to be oppositional. This is not to say that intentionally oppositional behavior does not exist. Rather, it is imperative to begin an assessment with the goal of making sense of behavior and identifying the factors relevant to that behavior. I think a sense of openness, or what psychotherapists with what is known as a postmodernist orientation sometimes call a "not-knowing stance," contributes to a richer understanding of children and what they are communicating through their actions. Ideally, it also allows for the formation of relationships founded on support rather than coercion.

Chapter 4

CONSTRUCTING BEHAVIORAL INTERVENTIONS: WHY WE NEED MORE THAN A TEMPLATE

PRINCIPLES OF BEHAVIOR PLANNING

In this book, behavior planning is viewed as a contributing change agent affecting behavior, cognition, and higher-level thinking skills—that is, the capacity to reflect on one's thinking. As such, there is an underlying educational component to the principles described here. Within this framework, the primary goal of behavior planning with children is to provide them concrete forms of *feedback*. Such feedback, if delivered effectively, should aid in the building of coping skills and the capacity for self-monitoring (or self-awareness). In simpler terms, children should gain new knowledge about themselves as the result of a behavioral intervention. In a school setting, the introduction of a behavioral plan also creates a structure that holds teachers and staff as accountable as students because the feedback must be consistent and generate an aura of predictability. In other words, it helps children learn how to understand, order, and anticipate their environment. The creative use of behavioral interventions, based on a sound understanding of children's disparate behaviors, avoids the emphasis on compliance and control favored by some systems.

Excerpts from Chapter 4 originally published in "Behavior Management Principles: Incorporating a Biopsychosocial Perspective," by James E. Levine, published in *Child & Adolescent Social Work Journal, 18,* no. 4. (August, 2001): 253–261. Reprinted with kind permission of Springer Science and Business Media.

The notion of applying positive reinforcement is certainly not new. Other models of behavioral intervention have adopted such an approach (Canter & Canter, 1992).[64] These prescriptive models, however, generally describe a methodology or set of positive practices without linking them to a larger theoretical orientation; that is, they are based on what works for practitioners in particular settings, often without regard to their meaning for the child, an understanding of his broader life circumstances, or our larger conceptual understanding of that child. In conjunction with developing new practice ideas, it is equally important that we aim to comprehend the connection between clinical interventions and the theories underlying our work. Furthermore, it is equally imperative that behavioral interventions, in practice, are applied in resourceful and flexible ways that resonate with the developmental needs of recipient children.

Accordingly, 10 principles for establishing successful behavior plans will be described, followed by case examples. Each principle rests on the core notion of behavior planning as a vehicle for providing feedback and helping children learn about their behavior.

1. Behavioral interventions must be positive. They should augment rather than replace limit-setting approaches or broader discipline codes, which provide structure for the individual and also reflect environmental goals. Their purpose is to promote mastery rather than a fear of failure because mastery of a task will ordinarily reduce the need for extrinsic forms of motivation. Put differently, it means that once children figure out how to accomplish something successfully, they usually do not need to be rewarded for it any longer. Clinicians are generally comfortable with the notion of mastery, given their strengths-based orientation and training (Saleebey, 1996).[65] In a similar vein, teachers are well versed in the idea that mastery of academic content leads to greater academic risk taking and engagement. Since the purpose of the behavioral model described in this book is to promote a better understanding of behavior, the parallel is clear: most children, if they experience new successes in their behavior, are in turn more willing to try out and commit to new strategies for ways to act both in school and at home.

2. Consistent with children's developmental need for self-determination and autonomy, they must be allowed to participate in devising the behavioral interventions that affect their day-to-day life in school. Although this may appear paradoxical, children are more likely to engage successfully in a behavioral plan if they are able to offer input into its development. This is especially true in terms of establishing the range of rewards that can be earned. In my experience, the act of imposing a child's behavioral plan typically rests on a philosophy of punishment and control. As a consequence, the child will fight the behavior plan to regain a sense of self-control. The confounding factor is that, since the child is denied the privileges that are made possible by the plan, he may become further enraged. A vicious cycle is established, with limited opportunity for a satisfying outcome.

I especially observe such a pattern in children with a history of trauma. The idea that we need to help combat children's sense of powerlessness, even in those whose behavior may be so challenging, can be a hard sell among overburdened teachers and counselors. Yet it is a primary factor as to whether children will buy in to this kind of intervention.

There are, of course, occasions in which a child may refuse to participate. In these instances, it is beneficial to explain the consequences for making such a choice. It is also helpful to allow time for the child to process the offer since many children are accustomed to summarily opposing any statement put forth by adults. Providing this in a manner that is most face-saving to children increases the likelihood that they will agree to contribute. Such a scenario once again points to the relational aspect of establishing a successful intervention.

3. Food should not be included as an option for reward. Such a notion is counter to a time-honored tradition in behavioral psychology, especially for those trained in the idea of M&Ms as the ultimate reinforcer. It is probably not a coincidence that a range of available rewards is known as a *menu,* which connotes the food orientation underlying many behavioral plans. There are compelling reasons to avoid food as a reinforcer. First, many children have been deprived of or denied adequate food. The issues such a scenario raises may be traumatizing; at the least, these may lead to highly distressed or explosive reactions. Food connotes a very basic and primary form of reinforcement and is too powerful to become a measured source of reward. Second, there are numerous children with obesity or various kinds of eating disorders, and the embellishment of food as a reward perpetuates these problems; that is, we often equate eating with *goodness,* a problematic connection commonly confronted by clinical practitioners in work with both children and adults. More generally, many of us eat to make ourselves feel better, so the idea that we should communicate to children that food—usually sweets—is how to reward oneself is not a healthy long-term approach.

Instead, rewards should be offered based on a developmental understanding of the particular child. Contrary to the expectations of many parents, teachers, and clinical practitioners, younger children typically prefer a special time with adults rather than tangible rewards (Hill,

Olympia, & Angelbuer, 1991).[66] Latency-age children often enjoy grab bag items such as stickers, pens, and colored markers. Adolescents tend to want privileges such as extra computer time or the opportunity to listen to music. The critical point is that children must participate in choosing their own rewards and perceive that they have some level of ownership of the process.

4. Behavioral plans should be clearly written out and incorporated into the child's daily schedule. Visual learners generally require written cues and other visual aids (pictures, charts, etc.) in their environment to make sense of task demands (Hallowell & Ratey, 1994).[67] As indicated in the previous chapter, visual cues are integral to success for many people. Children with ADHD need visual cuing as well but also benefit from help in breaking down and sequencing specific steps. Each of these objectives can be achieved by providing a written schedule for the day that, at the same time, allows a teacher or counselor to visually display the child's behavioral progress.

5. Consequences should be provided in school rather than by parents. The immediacy of rewards is critical to their success. Also, parents may be unable to follow through at home on information provided from school. The outcome in such a scenario may be disastrous for the child since the message is that school cannot be trusted or that adults represent a monolithic source of disappointment. To some extent, we need to help children compartmentalize their lives because traumatic experience or lack of success outside of school should not equate with poor behavior in school (and, conversely, children who struggle in school often need added support from home). For many children, school is a safe haven, the place where they can flourish in spite of issues that confront them elsewhere. Since consistency is a core element of a positive relationship with adults, this is most easily ensured if the school setting follows through on its own commitments.

An example of this principle is as follows: Tony, a 12-year-old boy with severe ADHD, was assigned a long-term project in school, historically the type of task that would generate anxiety and, due to his lack of organizational skills, pained failure. Yet, in this particular instance, he persevered: he completed the assignment in a high-quality way, brought the full product into school, and turned it in to his delighted teacher. His behavior plan had been set up such that rewards would be provided at home by his mother, and this was a shining example of a time in which he deserved one. Arriving at home with his brother, however, he "swatted" the younger boy because he had been annoying him both on the bus and during the walk to the house. As he closed the door behind him, his mother told him she would be "goddamned" before she would consider giving him his reward since he had just hit his brother. This was horrifying to Tony—and the end of the behavioral intervention since, inevitably, he no longer held any trust in it. Such a model is not only ineffective, it also confuses children and the issues they face. To reiterate, the *immediacy* of rewards is a variable that must be assessed when developing a behavioral intervention.

This does not suggest that parents are secondary or insignificant participants. Parents should sign off on all behavioral interventions and receive ongoing feedback as to how their child is faring. Parents may choose to provide an additional reward if the child has done well at school. Nonetheless, it is critical that schools are held accountable for running effective behavioral interventions. We expect the same level of responsibility from students and can model this in our own actions.

6. *Behavioral plans should not perpetuate the notion of solely good and bad behavior.* For many children, especially during adolescence, a prime developmental task is to reduce the tendency toward dichotomous, black-and-white thinking. Yet, paradoxically, many behavioral interventions imbue such thinking in children because they either fully reward the child for targeted positive behavior or they completely deny reward for unwanted behavior; that is, there is no nuance to the perception of children's behaviors. In my own experience, this seems especially true when adults feel angered or threatened by a child's actions and subsequently resort to measures of control; the outcome is often one of extreme polarization between child and adults. Clinicians, with their understanding of the equivalent importance of environment and individual, are ideally suited to gauge the effectiveness of a particular setting (and its participants) in its planning, development, and implementation of behavioral interventions.

An illustration of this principle follows: I observed Ray in a resource room that was overcrowded with 18 kids. A challenging 13-year-old in seventh grade, he reportedly disliked school and let everyone around him know it. Identified with various diagnoses over the years, a recent evaluation found only an oppositional defiant disorder along with a specific learning disability. He was also smart, able to think on his feet, and funny. His behavior plan was set up to address multiple behaviors, with the opportunity to earn a notation of success (or lack thereof) per period. This is a standard approach that I have witnessed in many schools. Watching the entire long-block class, however, it was apparent that Ray had ups and downs. There were times when his behavior was on target, respectful, and task directed. At other times, he engaged with kids around him and disrupted the flow of the classroom. At the end of the period, when the children had departed, the teacher acknowledged that she was unsure how to grade him on his behavior. She noted that there were days in which he was "horrible" in the beginning and then right on target toward the end, but the behavior plan left open only the possibility of a yes or no on his check sheet. Her struggle was whether to emphasize what went wrong or to accentuate the positive.

Eventually, we reduced the number of behavioral goals to sharpen the plan, as the lengthy list could be reduced to two clear goals: follow directions, and show respect for others. We also adapted the plan to build in additional feedback options that reflected his gradations of behavior. The model shown in chapter 5 provides one example of how to do this. In the short term, since the teacher was familiar with such a model, we built in the opportunity to earn up to a certain number of points per class that could then be tallied up toward a reward. This represented an honest appraisal of his behavior and a more accurate way to reflect it. As noted, an essential task is to illustrate for children the subtleties of their behavior, what works and what does not, based on their developmental abilities. Any behavioral intervention should advance this objective.

As discussed in the prior chapter, behavior plans should not build in extra rewards for so-called perfect days. This type of reward option promotes the idea that one should strive for such perfection, something that is impossible to maintain and unwittingly reinforces black-and-white thinking. If good enough behavior is the goal, this should be the message from adults, and additional rewards imply a different message.

7. *There must be planned obsolescence from the outset.* In other words, there must be specific criteria for ending the use of any behavior plan. It may seem an obvious point, yet interventions frequently lack definitive criteria for termination, such that a plan simply drifts into disuse. This is a poor model for children in terms of promoting the ideals of planning, consistency, and perseverance. In addition, if the underlying goal is to teach children about their behavior, then it is essential that they fully comprehend the objectives of the behavioral plan and have a well-defined picture of what is expected from them. A formal end to the written plan is an opportunity to review progress, and it signifies a success for the child.

8. *Children should generally be weaned from behavioral plans.* If one considers these interventions a form of structure and support for a child, then it makes sense to reduce the need for them according to the child's capacity, rather than abruptly terminating them. It also makes sense that, during periods of high stress, a child might benefit from briefly

reinstituting a previous behavioral plan. Children are typically the most effective measure for determining whether a behavioral plan should be discontinued. Often, a child will lose interest in the reward but maintain mastery of a behavior, which signifies that the plan is no longer necessary. As noted, behavioral interventions are seen as teaching tools in this model as opposed to mechanisms of control; by extension, such interventions are prevention focused rather than punitive reactions to children's behaviors. If a child can avert a behavior by employing self-reminders (the goal of most behavioral plans), the need for a formal plan is reduced or eliminated.

The notion of weaning a child off a behavioral intervention is illustrated in the following example: Richard, a 10-year-old diagnosed with ADHD and mild oppositional defiant disorder, used such a plan for three months with a focus on his impulsive behaviors. His father had died suddenly a year earlier in an accident. In many ways, Richard was an ideal candidate for this type of intervention since teachers generally liked him (in spite of his occasional defiance) and were attuned to the loss of his father. Notably, Richard's diagnoses were established prior to his father's death. He made rapid progress once the intervention was established, mainly because he wanted to please the adults around him, especially his teacher. As such, the nature of the relationship, which is a critical variable in how a child responds to this sort of intervention, was already a positive factor. The feedback was helpful to him, he earned more and more check marks, and he was motivated by the reward options and, increasingly, his mounting mastery of new behavioral skills. Even a boost to the number of required checks and the establishment of more stringent criteria to earn them did not create obstacles to his ability to succeed. After a period of continued achievement, the plan was discontinued, with fairly disastrous results. Richard was told about the change on a Friday, and by the end of Monday, he was already in the midst of a downward spiral. Staff were surprised by this outcome. It was, simply, too fast a change for him, as the continuous—and predictable—feedback had been an important component for helping him to monitor his behavior. While staff understandably saw the change as a triumph for him, he experienced it as a form of pulling out the rug from underneath him; that is, the support was withdrawn too hurriedly, and he crashed as a result. The plan was then reinstituted, and though it took a few days for Richard to calm down and regain his stride, he again made steady progress. At this point, a discussion was held about ways to gradually reduce the intervention. We developed a plan of action in which the frequency of feedback was slowly reduced. Instead of formally discussing his number of checks at the end of each period, this was initially cut back to every other period, with further decreases built in over time. For Richard, this was a much easier shift. He continued to earn rewards in this manner and, eventually, was able to discontinue the check sheet and simply review orally with the teacher how he had done. The provision of rewards was lessened from twice daily to once per day, and then further. Employing a gradual process, Richard was able to maintain his behavioral skills, though with some ups and downs. He also chose, at one point, to use the check sheet on a self- rather than other-monitored basis. What this example demonstrates is how behavioral interventions must be used flexibly, in support of and accounting for children's varying functioning levels and needs. It also points out that, just like academic concepts, children internalize and enact behavioral skills at different rates.

9. Behavioral plans are only one component of a concerted approach to helping. While this seems, on the surface, to be a simple comment, there are numerous instances in which schools employ them as alleged cures for behavioral issues. It is essential that children understand that they are viewed (and valued) as more than the sum of their discrete actions. Communicating a larger holistic perspective to children about their specific trouble-inducing behaviors raises the prospect that some space exists between a person's greater self and their behavior in the moment; it does not reduce the child's responsibility, but rather implies hopefulness and the potential for growth. As noted throughout this book, a behavioral intervention is more effective when implemented in the context of a caring, respectful relationship, reminiscent of Winnicott's conception of a *holding environment* (Applegate, 1997).[68] In simple terms, Applegate describes Winnicott's conception of a holding environment as one in which an individual experiences a sense of safety, similar to when a parent holds a child. It serves as a container for strong feelings. The feedback to a child concerning his behavior should, ideally, be provided in such an atmosphere of trust. Like other therapeutic approaches, the intent should be to help rather than punish the child.

10. The final principle is that, ultimately, behavioral interventions are not always successful. Such an outcome represents a range of possible meanings, and we need to assess the viability of each option. For instance, the plan may not be structurally sound, whether the goals are unattainable or incorrectly targeted, or the rewards are not motivating to the child. The plan may also not be consistently or effectively administered, such that the child gains little real feedback. It is especially not helpful, for example, if a child attains enough check marks to earn a reward but does so in an environment of hostility toward his achievement; this does little to promote constructive behavior. This also clarifies that behavioral interventions are more than just *technical* approaches within our repertoire of clinical methods.

A poor result may additionally reveal that the child cannot connect behavior to an outcome—this can be seen in children with particular neurological difficulties such as profound ADHD. Notably, such conditions are explanations for behavior, not excuses (Cooley, 1998).[69] This connection between actions and consequences can be taught as part of a social skills curriculum, especially ways in which to read and respond to environmental cues (McGinnis et al., 1984; their work has been updated and expanded since its inception).[70] Social skills training, as discussed in chapter 3, relies on the idea of teaching children new skills rather than assuming from the outset that all problematic behaviors are volitional and planned. A behavioral intervention has no chance for success if the child does not possess a clear sense of how to act or respond.

Notably, unsuccessful behavioral plans may indicate that a child's life is rooted in such disarray and chaos that a lone intervention does not offer enough structure and predictability to be of use. Ethically, this suggests that supplementary interventions are necessary and should be pursued. In addition, it reinforces the clinical mandate to attend to a wider set of biological, psychological, and social factors.

An example of the last principle, Tim, a 12-year-old with severe ADHD and specific learning difficulties, reported that he detested school and experienced the rules there as arbitrary and unfair. His description of himself was that he "lives in the moment," which, apparently, he had heard others say about him. Tim presented with difficulty in connecting his behavior to particular outcomes; it was as though, perceptually, he could not conceive of the link, at least not in the moment. When discussing the behavior of other children, he was able to articulate the association between actions and consequences, but he could not transfer this knowledge into comprehending his own behavior in the course of real-life situations. Moreover, he had overt social skills concerns, which had been reported since kindergarten. In essence, he moved so quickly through life that he missed social cues, especially those communicating that he needed to back off from others. This led to relationship issues, both in school and at home with his mother and siblings. Because of an intermittent seizure disorder, his mother did not feel comfortable in allowing him to use stimulant medication (because of the risk of his developing more seizures), and alternate choices, such as Strattera, did not work effectively for him. Many behavioral interventions had been tried without success, even though Tim was motivated by the reward options.

The plan depicted in Chapter 5 was then attempted and revealed that there was little pattern to his behavioral difficulties, other than that the less structured parts of his day were the most difficult for him. This was not a revelation to anyone working directly with Tim. Clearly the behavioral plan reflected his behavioral issues rather than ameliorated them. Since the plan was unsuccessful, the school discontinued it after three weeks and incorporated a number of other approaches. One—which would seem obvious on the surface but had not been employed since he moved repeatedly to different school districts—was to evaluate his learning. Because his behavior was consistently challenging, and he was an articulate, obviously bright boy, there had been little willingness or opportunity to assess his learning needs; that is, he had been viewed as socially maladjusted rather than as a child formally in need of services. When he was tested, surprising results emerged: he had a number of specific and severe learning needs that had gone unrecognized and unaddressed. The simple act of moving him into smaller resource room classes was helpful. Also beneficial was a social skills group held at his middle school. This was, in fact, so helpful to him that he was additionally enrolled in an outside skills group, something his school staff were astonished to discover that he enjoyed. With his confidence growing that he might finally experience some success, Tim engaged with an outside therapist, where he addressed cognitive approaches for stopping and thinking, rather than reacting to events. It was at this point that the behavioral plan was reinstituted, with dramatically different results. Tim was motivated by the regular feedback and understood that he needed to work to connect his behaviors with their logical outcomes. It was as though he was becoming conscious of cause and effect for the first time, in the way that a much younger child would, because this is where his developmental lag was most acute. Success was not a straight line on the graph; he had numerous ups and downs over the next few months, but the general trend was positive, and Tim reported that he felt optimistic that he would continue to improve. The school's attitude was one of hopefulness. As such, the *timing* for implementing the behavioral plan was a critical variable as it offered limited help at the outset but subsequently became an important feature of the overall strategy. What this case indicates, therefore, is that the behavioral intervention was one piece of a larger approach, not a solution in and of itself.

To illustrate the 10 principles further, another case discussion will follow that demonstrates the importance of a supportive environment in utilizing a behavioral intervention. Marco is 11 years old, an Italian, white, middle-class child living in a quiet, suburban community. Previously diagnosed with ADHD, it was recently determined that his symptoms were indicative of AS instead. Complaints about his behavior centered on his facial grimaces and his inability to keep his hands to himself when sitting in group activities. Furthermore, he was reported to be inattentive, impulsive, and rigid about changing activities or topics of discussion. Prior behavioral interventions targeted these behaviors and emphasized removing him from the group when he engaged in them. Generally, this led to furious reactions from Marco, who clearly did not wish to be excluded from his peers.

A new behavioral plan was developed. This emphasized success based on a number of criteria, such as on-task behavior and following directions. Marco participated in discussions concerning the goals of the plan and the rewards to be earned. Like many children his age, he chose extra computer time. Given the recent change in diagnosis to AS, and thus the new angle on making sense of his unusual behaviors, facial grimaces were now understood to mean that Marco was overstimulated by the group environment; similarly, his problem with touching other children was viewed as a matter of overstimulation since it occurred only during group activities, when he was amid the usual clamor of other fifth graders. To address these concerns, Marco was seated farther back from the group rather than removed; this empathic and very simple environmental intervention led to a substantial reduction in the occurrence of such behaviors. In addition, he was provided a daily schedule that incorporated visual reminders of the social rules he needed to follow. Fortunately, Marco attended a classroom with both a supportive teacher and a well-trained, insightful paraprofessional. In the context of these warm, attuned relationships, some of the reported rigidity began to diminish, and Marco exhibited better capacity to make transitions, stay on task, and follow directions. While he continued to adhere to his own unusual interests in an often repetitive fashion (consistent with mannerisms associated with AS), Marco made significant strides over a six-month period.

Rooted in a framework that encompasses biological, psychological, and social factors, behavioral interventions are most effective when utilized in positive and even compassionate ways. As they are typically designed, however, these interventions appear to hold a questionable reputation among many school staff and clinical practitioners. In the current managed care climate, a growing number of clinicians are pressured, if not mandated, to utilize such short-term approaches (Schamess, 1996).[71] For those—including, of course, parents—who operate in systems concentrating on children, it is imperative that behavioral practices personify a grasp of method and appreciation for children's changing developmental needs. All of these practices derive from understanding the importance of relationship and the meaning of behavior. Only when behavioral plans are viewed as a single component of intervention, rather than as a sufficient practice modality, are they effectively employed in the service of challenging children. As such, the biopsychosocial approach should not be subsumed by the need for behavioral interventions. Rather, such interventions must be anchored in an overarching understanding of the whole child.

Chapter 5

THE NUT AND BOLTS: DEVELOPING, INTRODUCING, AND IMPLEMENTING THE BEHAVIORAL MODEL

I have advocated that one must hold some kind of overriding theory about a child's behavior before selecting an approach to intervention. Exploring the meaning of particular behaviors is critical, as is understanding the broader context in which they occur. Without these steps, which are ideally constructed and enacted via meaningful relationships, adults' attempts to squelch the behavior will rest on power and coercion. While these attributes are necessary in some situations, they should not serve as a starting point for intervention. As such, the school-based model described here is defined for children (and their parents) as a concrete teaching tool, one that will help them with their behavior just as they are helped in school with developing their academic skills. This is not a small, throw-in comment: it is imperative that everyone involved in the process buy into the idea that the primary purpose for implementing these interventions is to teach children how to broaden their behavioral options and ways to make better choices.

The process of arriving at a working hypothesis about behavior is handled in various ways and referred to in different terms, but there seems to be a general pattern. Often called a child study team, the goal is to develop a protocol for discussing the needs of specific children. Some schools develop a referral form such that a good deal of thought has gone into what has and has not been successful, and the team can then brainstorm additional problem-solving ideas. The point is to bring together the observations of and strategies used by the teachers, the insights of the school counselor, and the thinking of other school staff involved with the child. Some schools invite parents to participate in a part of the process. Typically, this sort of review leads to new ideas and greater awareness that this is a child who requires additional vigilance. For children with more serious or complex needs, the FBA process discussed earlier in the book should be undertaken.

In my experience, there are usually a number of strategies to consider before the recommendation for a formal behavior plan should be made. These may take the form of ignoring particular behaviors, modifying the child's academic work, referring the child for counseling, and/or setting clear expectations and limits. An additional benefit to such teams is that, frankly, they are a forum for teachers to be heard concerning the difficulties of managing classroom behavior. It is essential for teachers to observe that other staff—counselors, various specialists, such as speech and occupational therapists, and, especially, administrators—are contributing to the process for devising helping approaches.

The model involves an extensive preteaching component, which means that the plan is not begun until the child has sat with relevant adults and fully grasped how the plan works. The goal of any behavioral intervention should be that, ideally, if the child is stopped in the hallway and asked to describe it, he could detail exactly how it operates and what it aims to help. This is often a primary weakness in how these interventions are utilized, as I come across innumerable children who cannot either articulate the goals of the plan or specify how it works. There may be a vague sense of rewards that will come about if a child is "good," but much more needs to be understood. In essence, the expectations must be clear, and the child should be able to state (or at least understand, if he will not talk about it) exactly what he needs to do to earn rewards. Equally, he should be able to discuss the process—that is, when he meets with a teacher to review his behavior, what they are likely to talk about, how that conversation will take place, and so on. How well the intervention is taught—which means it is a labor-intensive process at the outset—is a critical variable in determining its success, even though this seems to be an area given less attention both in the literature and in practice.

As noted, I prefer children to be involved in establishing both the goal setting and reward options. Any child placed on an individual behavior plan should understand that he has been given the opportunity to learn about and participate in it, given the larger mission for employing the plan in the first place—to teach the child about his behavior. Primarily, it is the process involved in giving consistent and honest feedback that creates the conditions for behavioral change. How this discussion transpires is a key variable in whether the plan is helpful. For some children, the chance to hold a real dialogue with adults sets a positive tone.

Moreover, it is essential to avoid a mechanistic use of the behavior plan. The preteaching segment, just as in all discussions of the plan once it has been instituted, should account for the temperament of and issues faced by the child. Is he defensive? Open to learning more about himself? Depressed? In legal difficulty? All these considerations must be factored in when attempting to engage a child in a discussion of the behavioral intervention and, ultimately, his behavior. Some children simply need extra time to come to the point where they can begin to look honestly and openly at their behavior.

In this model (Example 1), a beginning-middle-end format is used as this is instrumental in allowing children to observe their behavior in sequential order. One can clearly observe patterns of success and problem areas, especially because the model illuminates the distinctions between transitional periods and work-oriented phases. A hallmark of ADHD, for example, as any teacher or parent knows, is how suddenly things can fall apart during the transition between activities or locations. Given this, the model is not segmented into equal time components for each period; rather, it illustrates the (1) initial transition to starting an activity, (2) the bulk of the work period that follows, and (3) the final transition in terms of the point in time where a teacher asks her students to begin winding down and preparing for the next activity. While children with ADHD tend to struggle with transitions, children with learning disabilities may be more likely to experience difficulty during the work period itself. Check sheets can be utilized to discern such patterns. This approach tries to take into account that behaviors arise for different reasons and thus at different times.

The following (Example 2) is similar in layout but oriented to older students. It continues with the beginning-middle-end format but, visually, looks more like a kind of contract and tends to appeal to more mature students.

There are three steps in relation to the *language* of the plan. First is a *redirection,* which almost any experienced teacher or parent will employ. This is when the adult will repeat the direction, note someone else in the room who has successfully complied, or do something to alter the scenario ("Whoops, I dropped my pencil. Now then, Joe, what was it I just asked you to do?") to then return to the initial direction. It is more art than science, and any one or combination of these strategies may be more effective for different individuals. No challenge is issued to the

Example 1

Wednesday	Instruction	Beginning	Middle	End		Goal
8:40-9:15	MORNING ROUTINE				18	
9:15-9:45	MORNING MEETING				15	
9:45-10:30	READING WORKSHOP				12	
10:30-11:15	RESOURCE ROOM				9	
11:15-11:50	WRITING WORKSHOP				6	
11:50-12:00	HAND WASHING				3	
12:00-12:30	LUNCH				18	
12:30-1:00	RECESS				15	
1:00-1:15	READ ALOUD				12	
1:15-2:30	MATH				9	
2:30-3:00	LIBRARY				6	
3:00-3:15	DISMISSAL				3	

My goals for today are:

1)_____

2)_____

My rewards for today are:

1)_____

2)_____

Example 2

NAME: DATE:

BEHAVIOR CONTRACT

PERIOD/COMMENTS	Beginning	Middle	End
7:30–7:44 — Homeroom			
7:45–8:32 — First Period			
8:33–9:20 — Exploratory (Tu/Th = Fourth Period)			
9:21–10:08 — Second Period			
10:09–10:56 — Third Period (Health)			
10:57–11:57 — Fourth Period (Tu/Th = Gym/Swim)			
11:57–12:27 — Lunch			
12:28–1:15 — Fifth Period			
1:16–1:43 — Sixth Period			
1:44–2:03 — Art/Music/Other encore classes			
2:04–2:10 — Homeroom			

TOTAL NEEDED: TOTAL EARNED:

GOALS
1. Follow directions.
2. Be respectful to others.

child during this phase, and the behavioral plan is not invoked. Instead, the goal is simply to call the child's attention to the task at hand.

The second step is a *reminder*. This term was chosen carefully, and I prefer it because of its emphasis on joining with the child more so than the commonly used term *warning*. My experience is that warnings, especially for children with behavioral disorders, generally produce a warning in return. It is as though the gauntlet has been thrown, and adult and child are then locked into a power struggle. In this model, children are taught that a reminder is a code word reminding them that they need to comply with the goal. Adults have an equal responsibility here; we must clearly name the specific behavior we wish to see happen next. I have observed that many children, especially those with ADHD or other forms of sequencing problems, can formulate what they are *not* supposed to do but, conversely, cannot articulate or enact the particular action called for in the moment. Adults should clarify the next step in clear, concrete terms—this is a cardinal rule of the plan. Over the years, I have met with many teachers who were initially skeptical about this simple intervention but found it immensely useful when trying it.

For example, an eight-year-old boy, Keith, who was diagnosed with ADHD and oppositional defiant disorder, used a behavioral intervention to help him with blurting out in class, listening to directions, and making mildly rude comments. This is a boy for whom the act of sequencing was extremely difficult; even the retelling of a simple story left him all over the place when he would attempt to arrange and describe the details of the plot. His behavior followed a similar pattern, and he was often frustrated over his struggle to follow through or get things right. Observing him, I could see his spirits diminish in front of my eyes. In employing the behavioral intervention, his teacher was careful to emphasize the fact of what needed to happen next—in the moment, this was all that mattered. He needed to sit in his seat or sit quietly for a moment. His teacher retrained herself to simplify her language and reduce the amount of talk. She did not refer to consequences or describe the trouble he would bring on for himself if he did not comply. Instead, she repeated the instruction if Keith did not follow through the first time. All the child study team members involved with Keith were surprised by the effectiveness of this seemingly straightforward step.

The final step is an *earn* or *not earn* of the check mark. Check marks are preferable because they are neutral and less emotionally loaded than smile/frown faces, gold stars, stickers, and so on. This choice of terms is based on the values underlying the model; that is, it is critical that children see the power they hold over their own behavior. I do not take away check marks or fail children—the choice to earn or not earn check marks is theirs. Initial discussions concerning the plan emphasize such thinking, and the concept is continually stressed throughout its use. The only exception to the rule is in the event of overtly aggressive behavior. It makes little sense to reward a child who may have earned enough checks but then hurts someone. This exception is clearly discussed with children before starting the plan.

The behavior plan does not replace a school's discipline code; rather, it is an adjunct to it. This is a significant point that does not always receive enough attention when the idea of a behavioral intervention is put forth. Predictably, it often gets raised as a question by teachers and school counselors since a not-earn is clearly not enough of a consequence in response to serious behaviors. I always clarify with children and their parents that the plan is a way to help prevent problematic behaviors by teaching and reinforcing better ones—but a not-earn does not substitute for a trip to the principal or other school protocols if undesirable behaviors occur. Whether a particular behavior counts as an automatic not-earn should be determined by the developmental abilities of the child and what can reasonably be expected. A kindergartener who, for example, pushes in line might get a not-earn for that time block but would not be fully disqualified from earning his morning reward. Instead, I might invoke the one-arm's-length rule for such a child to help him define the necessary spatial boundaries.

In this model, I clarify that the initial commitment from children and their teachers is no longer than three weeks. This is an important point because, as indicated in the last chapter, behavioral interventions often drift off rather than systematically diminish toward a clear and unequivocal ending. The purpose for establishing a preliminary time limit is both to increase children's buy-in to the process and to build optimism on the part of adults. Many teachers express a negative reaction to such plans, especially ones that seemingly require a substantive commitment of time. Providing clear parameters from the outset and assuring staff that the plan is an assessment tool as well as a possible change agent often lessens the pressure in terms of expectations. It is, perhaps surprisingly, often the teacher who suggests we continue an intervention based on a child's improved behavior. If a plan is unsuccessful, an essential component of responsible practice is to review such an outcome and, as noted in chapter 3, develop a set of hypotheses as to why this is so. If the plan is subsequently modified in some way but continues to be ineffective, it may be that discontinuing it is the best choice at that particular moment. This needs to be explained to the child in a way that avoids blame and allows for the possibility of its reimplementation when possible.

Generally, it is helpful to start the plan with a 75 percent expectation for check marks to earn rewards, though this is certainly not a rigid figure. For children in elementary school, and even some children in middle school, it is important to start with twice-per-day rewards. Too many children with a history of behavioral failure have had the experience of blowing it by nine o'clock in the morning, which leaves no opportunity for them to turn their behavior around and thus to see that they can be concretely rewarded for that shift. Similarly, many teachers report that they are not as stringent with the criteria of the plan because they want to avoid such a situation. Knowing that there is an additional time period in which a child can earn a reward reduces the pressure on everyone. I have continually encouraged children to try to turn it around, and this is a key component of the model's language and approach.

Typically, I promote reward options that link comfortably with the flow of the particular classroom. If events are hectic at the end of a fourth grader's day, it may be that a simple grab bag filled with markers, pens, colored erasers, baseball cards, and so on can be employed before the child races out to the bus. The midday reward could be a book, computer access, or time to draw—that is, something that will be calming for the child and reduce his overall level of stimulation. It is 10 minutes well worth granting. Equally imperative is the need to make certain that the rewards are developmentally accurate and, as noted, consist of options that the child finds motivating. When using rewards twice a day, I have found it important to ensure that the same reward is not offered in both instances as it tends to lose its luster fairly quickly. This may sound obvious, but a number of children (those with AS, for instance) tend to choose the same reward, such as time at the computer. Similarly, the available reinforcers may need to be switched if their effect seems to be wearing off. These types of considerations should be addressed during the preteaching segment of the intervention, though they can be raised again during a periodic review of how the plan is proceeding from the child's perspective.

The rationale for including what looks like a bar graph or thermometer on the right-hand side of the chart is that many younger children—and some who are older—lack a grasp of number concepts such that they cannot make sense of their growth. The graph serves as a visual representation of this. Many children enjoy drawing in their progress, which requires no additional time but is another way to invest them in the process. The purpose of this visual guide, consistent with the larger discussion of the model, is to teach productive behavior, and strategies that advance this purpose are worthy of inclusion. Example 1 provides a sample illustration of the bar graph.

A frequently asked question during my consultation meetings is what to do when a child has earned enough checks to gain a reward and then slacks off at that point. Children often quickly recognize the possibility of such a scenario. In general, I congratulate the child on having this level of awareness (he did, after all, discover the seams in the plan) and suggest that he is ready for me to raise the ante. Whether this means that the number of checks needs to be increased and/or that the criteria for earning them need to become more stringent should be explored by members of the team. In some situations, I have modified the plan such that children need to earn either the final check of the day or two of the last three; that is, we build in the requirement for the child to have a successful end to his day, especially when it is evident that the child has full control over this. The purpose is to set appropriate limits and communicate that one recognizes the growing level of volition the child holds over his behavior. For some children, paradoxically, this end-of-day drop-off in behavior—as long as it is a temporary and relatively benign occurrence—represents an event worth celebrating.

An additional question that often emerges is what to do when a child continues to be motivated by earning check marks, is invested in the feedback process, but no longer seems to care about the rewards, even if alternative choices are made available. Not surprisingly, this scenario is one to which we should aspire. The child is exhibiting a shift from needing extrinsic rewards to altering his behavior based on developing internal mastery—this is precisely the goal of the behavior plan. As noted in the last chapter, such a scenario signifies that it may be time to formally wean the plan such that rewards are secondary to the feedback process. One option is to slowly decrease the frequency of rewards, and another is to discontinue the need for earning checks to gain the reward; that is, the reward can be based on an informal judgment of how the child is doing rather than on a particular number of earned check marks. Or, conversely, a self-monitoring of the plan may be possible. The point is that, at this point in the process, the rewards hold less significance than the child's growing sense of mastery. Typically, a child has made significant progress when an issue like this is raised as a consult question.

FEEDBACK

Feedback to the child is given at the end of each allotted time period, focusing on the three separate phases. Such feedback must be consistent and timely. Teachers sometimes express understandable concern about having to meet so regularly with the child. Yet the amount of time devoted to a child who requires a behavior plan is inherently substantial; I am clear in expressing that this upfront commitment should progressively save time. As noted, I am equally clear in stating that the plan should only be in place for approximately two to three weeks if it is not contributing to more productive behavior.

Feedback as an overarching concept receives surprisingly little attention in terms of both its importance and the process for utilizing it. I have seen virtually no discussion of this in the literature on behavioral interventions. Yet it is one of the integral variables in whether the plan will be successful. Clearly *how* feedback is given—whether, for example, it is done in a supportive, encouraging way—is embedded in a larger relational matrix such as the quality of the relationship between adult and child. Miller and Rollnick (2002), describing a psychotherapeutic approach they call *motivational interviewing,* depict an approach for engaging reluctant clients in mental health services.[72] They delineate four main processes: elaborating client understanding, reflecting back to clients, summarizing ideas, and providing affirmation. These are not complicated notions, but they require careful listening, a nonjudgmental stance, and the emotional capacity to stay attuned to what clients are saying about their experience. Such strategies should be incorporated into the feedback process with children using behavioral interventions. The second case example later in this chapter shows how this might be done.

If we return to the discussion from early in the book concerning operant conditioning, it is not hard to extrapolate how essential a role feedback might play in determining whether a specific behavioral intervention is successful. As stated, operant conditioning is based on a simple stimulus-response model. Cognitive behavior therapy contributed the idea of cognition as an intervening factor, which includes mental processes such as our assumptions and thoughts. The feedback from a trusted adult should, of course, challenge a child's automatic assumptions and, when successful, alter some of how he understands his behavior. It serves, therefore, as a kind of mediating factor between a real-life precipitating event and the resulting behavior.

This notion attempts to tie together the practical act of implementing behavioral interventions with a larger theoretical perspective concerning the interplay between social relatedness and cognitive development and its impact on behavior. Behavioral interventions may or may not work in specific instances, but we must expand our level of knowledge with respect to what actually takes place in the process. Additionally, we need to advance our understanding of what underlies behavioral change. Feedback—or, more simply, how adults talk with children—is seen here as an integral factor.

Equally important is the need to be aware of the meaning of such feedback for the child. The level of praise should be geared to what a child can tolerate. Just as a negative, pessimistic style of interacting with a child can be damaging, a too effusive approach to giving praise can lead to a child who acts out to regain familiar ground. Ideally, the child can be invited to explore this with the adult, even if he cannot offer concrete suggestions as to the best ways to give him feedback. (Most children, for example, hate when it is done publicly.) Nonetheless, it is important to ask. The process of holding such a discussion provides children with a glimpse into how they can be viewed respectfully and in partnership around their behavior.

I met with a quiet, severely withdrawn 10-year-old boy, Earl, who had episodes of explosive anger. A seemingly small issue, no doubt the proverbial straw in whatever was going on for him up to then would evolve into his shouting, swearing, and turning over desks. These events led to his assignment to a behavioral classroom at school and, eventually, therapy with me. To say that this was a boy with low self-worth and a poor self-concept does not do justice to how badly he felt about himself and, at times, toward others. There was no obvious pattern to his outbursts, even when he transitioned into this substantially separate alternative classroom. The only pattern at all was that many of these outbursts appeared to come out of the blue. Earl finally provided me with the necessary insight to figure out a possible way to deal with this situation. He noted that classroom compliments from a teacher made him "ashamed," an astute reflection consistent with the fact that he had been bullied by his older brothers and eventually abandoned by his parents. Being good had not been helpful to him. He did not experience classroom comments intended to be affirming as a sign of his progress; rather, he viewed them as threatening and worrisome. Earl did not "know the kid they were talking about" and would act out to reduce the anxiety associated with this. Thus I asked his new teachers to check with him as to how he might want to receive praise, explain what it means, and review the process with him regularly. It also became a theme of therapy. Over time, in fits and starts, Earl learned how to put praise in a different perspective and accept it—if given privately—as worthwhile and even fairly comforting.

Finally, another factor to consider in relation to the notion of feedback is the amount of time allotted to the process. The goal is to provide children with the same commitment of time, whether their behavior is on target or not. My feedback is usually confined to one or two minutes, as there is much that can be said during this short period. The idea is to respond directly, concretely, and in a way that engages the child around the specific and agreed-on behavioral goals. I have observed that, in many instances, children receive more attention for what they have done wrong. Typically, there is greater detail and clarity attached to the description of what occurred. Moreover, children who display attention-motivated behavior often quickly grasp that they get more of what they want by acting out; this point was clarified for me by a young girl who was surprised that every adult does not "get it."

Conversely, when a child's behavior has met the goals of the plan, there may be a cursory, less enthusiastic acknowledgment of those actions. This same girl—bright, intuitive, and angry—told me that when she did well on her long-standing behavior plan, she received a perfunctory reply of "good work." It had no meaning for her at all. The approach proposed here stems from the idea that if a child is doing well, she will receive positive, descriptive feedback on a regular basis. It is imperative that children, especially those who have struggled behaviorally, develop a language for recognizing, understanding, and internalizing what they do well.

The following is an example of how the plan can be introduced and utilized. It involves Bob, a fourth grader with ADHD and various behavioral concerns. Bob was identified as a challenging child as early as kindergarten, when he had been unable to sit in circle, keep his hands to himself, or wait his turn to speak. These types of impulsive behaviors, along with his continual movement around the classroom and his seeming resistance to adult directions, contributed to almost constant difficulties in school. The same behaviors, in conjunction with increasingly evident signs of anger (fighting with peers, arguing with teachers) and his development of a limited number of friendships, have continued up to the current time. This presentation is certainly familiar to adults working in school settings and, of course, to parents of such children. Medication had been attempted and quickly discontinued by Bob's parents, who believed that stimulants and other types of medication were unwarranted in treating children. Some attempts at implementing behavioral interventions had been made, but these appeared to be inconsistent and unclear in their goals. The following excerpt is based on a conversation with Bob concerning the behavioral model described in this book. His teacher and school counselor were present for the discussion.

STAFF: Bob, we've noticed that you've been having some difficulty with the things we talked about before, like following teacher directions and making more respectful comments to other students. We've been thinking that it would make sense to try and help you in a more direct way with some of these behaviors. Would you agree that it's been hard for you?

BOB: *[Nods yes and looks away.]*

STAFF: Are there things that you feel have been going well?

BOB: I'm doing well in reading.

STAFF: Absolutely. You've done some nice work there and in some of your other classes. It seems like you've been trying really hard. How about in terms of your behavior—are there ways in which you've been successful?

BOB: *[Looks somewhat blank.]* No. I'm in trouble almost all the time.

STAFF: That's what we want to help you with. We'd like to use a chart as a way to show you what's working and what isn't. I know you've used charts before, but this is a different way of using them. Do you have any suggestions for what we should focus on?

BOB: No. Well, maybe how I get along with kids. Whatever.

STAFF: That's a good thought. Let's do that. We can set up a goal that focuses on getting along with other students by emphasizing saying nice things rather than things that make people mad. How about if we add one other goal about following directions?

BOB: *[Nods but does not say anything for a moment.]* Okay.

A discussion then ensued about rewards. Because he is artistic, it was an almost obvious choice that he would choose time to draw. Bob wanted this for the midday reward period, which came just before lunch. For the end-of-day reward, he was initially not interested in choosing from a grab bag but instead wanted 10 minutes to get a start on his homework. His teacher felt this could not be promised him on a daily basis. They agreed that if it was not available on a particular day, Bob would choose from the grab bag, especially if baseball cards were one of the options. At first, Bob denied that he wanted to earn time with a favorite adult, but he then slyly noted that if his teacher "wants to have lunch with me once in a while, I'd think about it." It was left that this would be an occasional option if Bob wanted it and his teacher had time available to stay in the classroom with him and a chosen friend.

The next excerpt illustrates the language of the plan as it was utilized in the classroom. The situation is one in which Bob has been fidgety since he stepped into the classroom, and it is now the first-period English class. He has had difficulty putting his things away, placing his homework in the appropriate location, and avoiding rude exchanges with a couple of classmates.

> TEACHER: Everyone, please take your seats and get out your materials for English class. *[She waits a couple of moments.]* Bob, I know I'm a bit hoarse and hard to hear, but why don't you grab a seat. Jenny, I can see you have everything out for class. Thanks. Good idea to bring out your *DEAR* [Drop Everything and Read] book, too. Great. *[Bob is still fumbling in the corner, sharpening his pencil and looking over at another student.]* Hey, Bob, what did I ask you to do?
>
> BOB: *[Looks sullenly at her. He does not make any motion toward his seat. He says nothing and turns back to the pencil sharpener.]*
>
> TEACHER: Bob, here's your reminder. I need you in your seat because I'm about to begin, and I don't want you to miss the directions.
>
> BOB: *[Grudgingly moves over to his desk and looks up at her. While he continues to look angry, he complies with her directive.]*

Bob required a reminder during the middle of the period because he began to make unnecessary comments as part of a short classroom discussion about a book the students had been assigned. The initial redirection was not successful, but the formal reminder was enough to help Bob rein himself in. During the transition at the end of the period, however, Bob began to make more negative comments, and the reminder did not alter this behavior. As such, he was given a not-earn for the final third of the period. Here is a look at the feedback that followed.

TEACHER: How do you think you did this period?

BOB: I . . . *[Looks down.]* I don't have much to say about this period. I had things on my mind.

TEACHER: It's fine to have things on your mind. Even if they are things that are bugging you. But you still need to concentrate and do your best. You know what I saw, Bob? I saw a fourth grader who was working really hard to stay in control of himself. For the most part—at least during the first two blocks of the class—you did that. I had to give you one reminder, but you were able to turn yourself around. It didn't look like it was easy, but you did it. Maybe you took a deep breath or something, I don't know. What I did see was that you put your feet on the floor, your body square in the chair, and your eyes up here on me. Whatever you used to help you, it wasn't there during the third block. That's when you made comments that might have been seen as disrespectful. Did you notice that as well?

BOB: *[Nods.]* Sometimes my mouth goes off before my brain does.

TEACHER: It's good to be aware of that. You'll get better at this— I've seen improvement from you. And you know, as difficult as that class was, you still earned two of your three checks, and you didn't argue when I told you that you'd gotten a not-earn. Whatever you did to help yourself, please do more of the same next period. Okay? If something is bothering you and you want to talk it over, you know you can ask for some time to go see the counselor.

BOB: *[Nods again.]*

The amount of time allotted to giving Bob this feedback was under a minute, yet it was positive in many ways. Most of all, it encouraged Bob to reflect on his behavior, named what he had done, and reminded him of his coping strategies. The teacher did not badger or threaten him; rather, she clarified what was not acceptable behavior. In observing this exchange, one could see that Bob was comfortable in accepting feedback from his teacher. He was not averse to hearing from her, which, given his history, was already a vast improvement in his way of interacting with adults. The relational aspects of implementing a behavioral plan are often ignored, yet they play a pivotal role in whether or not the intervention is perceived as a helping tool by the child.

Certainly there are times when a behavioral intervention will be unsuccessful. As noted, it is imperative to attempt to make sense of such an outcome. Ideally, the scenario is that, prior to implementing the behavior plan, the teacher has established a strong enough connection with the student that there is some consensus over what, together, they are trying to accomplish. Or, if the personal connection is lacking, one hopes that the teacher holds a reasoned assumption about what underlies the child's presenting behavior. Without this, there is generally a coercive tone to the plan that in a public school setting often does not work. If fourth grader Bob, for example, had not "grudgingly" moved back to his desk when asked, his teacher had other choices aside from the behavior plan. She could have chosen to ignore the behavior for a short while to see whether Bob returned to his desk on his own (that is, to determine if the behavior was attention seeking); she might have made a humorous comment about the dullness of the pencil point (I have witnessed teachers do this sort of redirection beautifully); or she may have chosen to invoke his risk in bringing about a visit to the principal (limit setting). Again, this choice would be driven by her understanding of Bob's recalcitrant behavior and what she believes it means in the moment—and, of course, what she thinks will work. Such a situation again points out that any behavioral intervention is only one component of a broader set of strategies for dealing with challenging behavior.

Many possibilities exist as to why behavior plans do not work in certain situations. For example, children with severe brain injuries (known more formally as TBIs) may not be affected by the idea of impending consequences. Many of these children live in the moment and do not necessarily connect current behavior with subsequent consequences, similar to the depiction in the previous chapter of Tim, an adolescent with ADHD. As such, they require different approaches such as preparation for events, self-calming techniques, questions rather than directives about consequences (this was discussed in chapter 2), and so on. A behavioral intervention may be more effective after these approaches have been instituted. Children with trauma histories often do not respond well to behavior plans until their sense of personal safety and capacity to adequately anticipate events (predictability) has been established. Similarly, explosive children, especially those for whom this is an intermittent and infrequent occurrence, need additional components built into their programs beyond behavior plans. As noted earlier, children with severe anxiety may be helped by a consistent behavior plan, but they typically require supplementary interventions as well such as teaching them self-calming strategies. Behavioral interventions must be adapted and utilized in ways that will supply a needed level of support.

In addition, there is a larger conversation that needs to take place when discussing specific school-based strategies such as behavior plans. Financial and, as a consequence, staff resources are a concern in almost every school district across the country, and any teacher with multiple behaviorally involved children in her classroom will point to this as a factor. No one should deny the commitment of time as well as the emotional investment and relational intensity involved in implementing a behavioral intervention, which is especially true if there is more than a single child who requires one and not enough adults in the classroom to participate. Frequently, teachers report that they do not want to institute such plans because of their fear that it would be impossible to adhere to the consistent schedule of feedback meetings with children. Yet, as I have pointed out throughout the book, the children who require behavioral interventions take up an excessive amount of teacher time and attention to begin with, and the behavior plan is one well-defined, time-limited, and systematic strategy for trying to ameliorate this. Moreover, they provide clear data for what is and what is not working.

Effective behavior management does not—and should not—rest solely with the classroom teacher. Administrators have a prominent role in supporting the plan, whether they are interacting with children, their parents, or the wider school community. Like many aspects of daily life in schools, these kinds of interventions work best when there is leadership backing for them. In such situations, for example, children may find the school principal checking in with them to gauge their progress, which only strengthens the power and significance of the intervention. Some children take great pride in sharing the news of their progress with other important people in their lives, and this serves as a kind of additional social reward.

The following is another example of how to implement the behavioral model described earlier in the chapter. Jason, a sixth grader with a history of depression and defiant behavior, was viewed by many adults in his school as a child who "just does not care," whether one was referring to his academic work or his relationships with teachers and other students. If I had been able to ask him directly—and he was willing to answer—my guess is that he would have put things in this very same way: he had essentially given up completely. People were worn down by his challenging behavior, unwillingness to follow directions, and generally poor attitude, though he was never overtly aggressive or violent. It was more a matter of irritability, an edge that came through in every comment and facial expression. Notably, trauma had been ruled out as an applicable diagnosis. To be frank, most seemed to doubt that depression was part of the equation, even though it was diagnosed early in grade school and then reconfirmed during the beginning of the school year. As discussed in chapter 2, it was difficult for teachers to accept that someone could be so disagreeable when depressed as they expected more in the way of obvious sadness. Informally, many adults perceived him as entitled, with an innate behavior problem to go along with his lack of motivation. In observing Jason, sadness was not part of his visible repertoire. His singular passion was computers, and this was both an area of interest and expertise for him, although he played it down when asked. Otherwise, he "hated" school.

Given this background, here is a snippet concerning his use of the behavioral intervention. He had not wanted to participate in a discussion of the rewards but was finally persuaded by his school counselor.

COUNSELOR: What kinds of things would interest you when you earn it on the contract?

JASON: *[Says nothing, with a sour look. Then he shrugs.]* Don't know and don't really care. You know?

COUNSELOR: Well, I know that you'll be dealing with this contract one way or another. You might as well make it into something you want.

JASON: C'mon, I've been on a million of these things. They haven't changed a thing.

COUNSELOR: Fair enough. But has anyone asked you about it before? I mean, has anyone actually included you as to how it should work and what you can earn?

JASON: No.

COUNSELOR: So this is a different gig. You're not a third grader anymore, and things are different. You have a chance to put your own two cents' worth into this. You might as well take advantage of it.

JASON: *[Looks away, but nods slightly in agreement.]* What are my choices?

COUNSELOR: There are a lot of things you can earn. Computer time, for one thing. You may be able to do some programming for the school if you want. Or you can play some (limited) video games. Occasionally, a no-homework pass if you want. Like I said, a lot of choices, but you have to weigh in or someone else makes the decision for you.

JASON: Done. I'll take the computer any chance I can get. Anything is better than my stupid classes.

Initially, Jason engaged reluctantly in the plan. It was as though it was outside of his experience to have a positive relationship with adults, and there were times when this seemed to threaten him; he would withdraw and become sullen, or instead take on an "I can't believe what an idiot you all are" look. At times his performance on the behavior plan was commensurate with his level of depression. A careful look at the data, along with periodic interviewing of staff, reflected all this. Jason would do well for a short time and then drop off suddenly and without any apparent reason. His homeroom teacher, who had him in class for two other subjects as well, finally noted this pattern for him on a day when he had been, in her terms, "really tough to deal with." The result was rather stunning in that Jason had been completely unaware of it. They also discussed a primary aspect of the plan—"You're not doing this for us, you're doing it for you"—and this finally began to make sense to him. He had always perceived the act of doing well as representing something only to please others, and this was plainly not his objective. What emerged over time is that he did not grasp his own successes or potential, traits that are consistent with depression. He also had little capacity to consider the future since he put vast energy into surviving the current moment, another characteristic often seen in people with depression.

The behavioral intervention was a spur in particular ways. The cause and effect of doing well in a way that benefited him directly seemed like a revelation to him. Perhaps it was the clear link between his two goals (following teacher directions and being respectful to others) and the reward outcome, but my own sense is that others had attempted to provide him with some level of consistency in the past. Instead, it may have been the overall constancy—including the regular feedback about his behavior—that helped him grasp this link. It also involved a genuine (if somewhat patchy) relationship with adults who, maybe for the first time, were willing to suspend some of their old assumptions and respond to him as a depressed, hurting child. When the plan was first introduced to teachers and administrators, I needed to assure them that there was a three-week statute of limitations if it was not successful. When they began to glimpse some forward movement in Jason, they no longer required any guarantees from me.

The fact that these different facets of the overall approach could be counted on was a new experience for Jason, even though he did not see that it was some of his own change in attitude and behavior that elicited a different sort of reaction from others. When the behavior plan is successful, I have often witnessed this kind of reciprocating pattern of change; that is, the child takes a positive step, others respond with encouragement, and a constructive cycle begins. This is, of course, the converse of the negative spiral that can envelope children struggling in school and/or at home.

As noted, the consistent feedback intrinsic to this approach was instrumental in helping Jason with his discoveries. His progress was uneven but, overall, showed good growth. His academic output improved. Most of all, he seemed to develop better relationships with his teachers, although, at least initially, there was limited change in how he interacted with peers. His trust did not extend that far. Fortunately, the computer time was indeed motivating, and this helped him during the rougher periods, especially when his mood—as he later put it—"went south." A nice addendum to the story is that Jason was so masterful at using computers that the school later "hired" him to do some training for staff and, on a few other occasions, to tutor students. It was therefore a combination of interventions—including the behavior plan—that helped him adjust to and cope more effectively with the demands of school.

CLASSROOM BEHAVIOR PLANS

Teachers and school counselors often ask about the use of classroom-wide behavioral interventions instead of individual plans, contending that they save time and serve the needs of a greater number of students. These can be a useful strategy for many children, and countless teachers are comfortable in applying such a model. The use of marble jars, classroom stickers or so-called bonus bucks, and weekly or monthly videos/outings/pizza parties all qualify as positive behavioral support for the classroom as a whole.

The difficulty lies in the fact that not all children are motivated by a successful outcome for the entire class, which means that peer pressure, rather than serving as an incentive, can become an impetus for acting out against the group. I have witnessed children become targeted by others in a classroom when they were viewed as the obstacle to rewards. Similarly, it is not unique that a class with two or more students with severely oppositional behavior might discover that these students coalesce against the behavioral expectations of the classroom, which puts them further at odds with their peers. At times, it creates a negative and self-perpetuating subculture within the classroom. This is not to condemn the notion of group interventions, as these can be highly motivating and successful, but it is imperative to make note of their limitations and the fact that they are not always a substitute for individualized behavior plans.

A specific classroom-wide model I have utilized is one in which the teacher freezes the class at random moments during a day. This works especially well with elementary school children but can similarly be employed with older students. The teacher has everyone stop without prior warning and then engages students in a review of their behavior. If they are on-task and meeting the agreed-on goals, they can earn points (or beans, or marbles, or anything that will motivate this particular group of students) that build toward an all-class reward. Younger children usually require a greater number of stopping points over the course of a school day—at least initially—to comprehend how this intervention works. They also need more immediacy in receiving the reward until they acclimate to such an intervention, while older students can typically wait somewhat longer; this needs to be determined based on the composition of the class, including their developmental levels, maturity, and capacity to wait.

The teacher may decide to vary the frequency for providing reward, which incorporates an element of unpredictability to the plan. This works better for some groups than others, based on whether they are oriented to finding it stimulating as opposed to disconcerting. Essentially, this functions as an intermittent model of reinforcement that can increase its power as a classroom tool. The allure of gambling is similarly reliant on the influence of intermittent reinforcement, which uses a variable frequency of rewards to increase their potency.

Another benefit of such a classroom-based intervention is that it builds in a series of reflective moments during the day, an important model for children that, for some, introduces the concept in a concrete and supported way. I have offered this same approach to parents in situations that involve more than one child in the home and a tendency for things to regress to an out-of-control level. Like teachers, parents sometimes feel comfortable in adopting this intervention because it addresses an entire group of children and, at the same time, they can choose when to stop the action. It does not need to be done on a set schedule or at a particular time, but does require a certain degree of intuitive skill at knowing how and when to interrupt the group and shift them into a more introspective process.

INDIVIDUAL BEHAVIOR PLANS
THAT USE SMILEY FACES

Schools frequently employ behavioral interventions that rely on stickers with facial expressions to provide feedback to children, especially those in early childhood classrooms. A common approach is to have a happy face, a neutral face, and one with a rather stern, disapproving expression as options. While some children can make good use of such interventions (and, as always, how the plan is implemented and what the relationship is like between child and adult are critical variables), others respond poorly. There are a few issues to consider in choosing this format. First, does the child understand facial expressions? Children on the autistic spectrum, for example, often do not grasp the nuances of these and thus may not respond differentially to them. Other children, especially those with trauma histories, may be frightened by the unhappy faces, and many have shared stories about how angry and rejecting these faces appear to them. Finally, some children are confused by the inscrutable "neutral" faces and perceive them as scary because they cannot make sense of them. Teachers and school counselors sometimes tell stories about children who experience these expressions as more disagreeable than the overtly unsmiling faces.

While the visual nature of this well-intended model makes sense from a developmental standpoint, it strikes me as a generally unhelpful design. I have listened over and over to children who believe that adults do not like them if their behavior is "bad." Some children describe what could only be construed as a deep sense of shame when they receive the unhappy faces. This then becomes an especially complicated teaching task when there is such a strong degree of social disapproval promoted via the behavioral intervention; that is, children may sense that they are not cared for (or even loved) if they act in challenging ways, certainly not the intended purpose for instituting a behavioral intervention. Virtually any self-help book or guide about children stresses the importance of distinguishing the child's behavior from his worth as a person. At times it is described in terms of separating the behavior from the child. Yet, for some children, this approach erases that crucial distinction and, on a practical level, does nothing to improve behavior. In spite of this perspective, many schools, agencies, and parents utilize such an intervention. Some children do well as a result, but my impression is that other approaches would work equally if not better for this group. And the potential damage it can inflict on the rest is substantial.

Instead, a simple behavior plan that uses clearly defined language, goals that make sense to the child, and visuals such as animal (or other types of) stickers for rewards is generally a better fit. I use the model described earlier in the book, and most children are excited by the thermometer and the opportunity to watch their success. In addition, any behavior plan used with young children requires frequent rewards until they have a firm grasp of how the intervention works in practice. The formal behavioral language applied to this process refers to it as the *density of rewards*. What it means in reality is that some children take longer than others to understand or respond to a behavioral intervention, and we may need to experiment with how often to provide rewards. As indicated in chapter 3, there are occasions in which we must be flexible to help inflexible children.

LEVEL SYSTEMS

In brief, another form of behavioral intervention is the level system. Typically found in classrooms for children with behavioral disorders, it is implemented in broadly different ways, but thematically, it consists of increasing tiers of rewards based on positive behavior. Often, in classrooms for older students, these rewards consist of privileges such as off-campus lunch or other opportunities for greater independence. In one school district, children of all ages with behavioral disorders are monitored through the hallways until they reach a particular level. If they drop down below a defined level, the typical protocol is to lose the assigned privileges. For younger children, various levels may signify different reward options such as access to a school store, time on the computer, homework passes, or the opportunity to play a game with peers. The premise is simply that children earn their way up or down in level, depending on their behavior. Ideally, the level system is individualized so that the feedback to each child is based on clearly defined behavioral goals.

Such interventions are implemented with varying degrees of success. Aside from the personal characteristics of a specific child, there are variables in terms of the technical usage of the plan. I have observed school programs in which points are dispersed somewhat randomly and without clear criteria. Moreover, the rewards may lack immediacy. Children will not be motivated by rewards experienced as disconnected from their behavior in the moment. As noted, this is both a developmental and temperament issue, and rewards must be in accordance with each. Finally, such behavioral systems should be consistent with the same principles described earlier in the book. Especially important is the idea that these interventions should be employed as a way to teach children about their behavior and reduce negative occurrences; they are not effective—or ethical—when used reactively in the guise of punishing children.

SAFETY PLANS

Another aspect of behavioral interventions, especially for children with difficulty managing angry behavior, is a safety or crisis plan. This is a kind of continuation of the behavior plan in that it is set in motion if a child becomes escalated to the point where there are—or may be—risks to his or others' safety. Typically, a safety plan is developed by the child study team or, in some situations, the school's crisis team. The purpose is to establish a clear, step-by-step protocol that specifies different adults' functions and roles. There are children whose level of rageful behavior can become dangerous to the extent that the police may need to be called. If such a risk exists, this needs to be written into the safety plan. Similar to a behavioral intervention, these plans should be signed off by parents and, depending on age and developmental level, the child as well. Either way, children should be aware of the plan and how it works.

It is useful to think of school-based interventions as being on a continuum rather than as a set of either-or approaches. Prevention is the key, and most of the strategies described in chapter 3 are based on the idea of averting problems before they occur. Behavioral interventions are, similarly, an attempt to teach children to avoid the pitfalls that lead to concerning behaviors. Numerous children respond favorably to such strategies, but if they surpass a certain threshold for frustration or stimulation, they may have difficulty pulling themselves back together, and their behavior can plummet quickly. Other strategies are more reactive in nature, such as safety plans, but they are also necessary in situations such as this. Understanding that a range of interventions may be needed, and identifying children who require such intensive help, will help schools in their planning and ability to respond both effectively and sensitively.

An example concerns Phil, 12 years old and in fifth grade. Already diagnosed with mild but global cognitive delays, he incurred a severe head injury during second grade when he fell off a fence. The accident resulted in seizures, time in the hospital, and retention in second grade. Recent neurological reports revealed that the injury is primarily healed, and there has been no seizure activity for more than two years. His developmental history includes a continuing diagnosis of intermittent explosive disorder. This had an early start, as he reportedly displayed major tantrums before the age of two. A complicated family history also affected his development and capacity to manage strong emotions, especially anger. Preventive techniques focused on helping Phil to recognize his pattern of escalation and request breaks when he felt he needed them. Since he preferred to perceive himself as no different than other children, he did not try to take advantage of the agreement by leaving class unnecessarily. Redirection was a useful strategy often applied successfully by his teacher, as was an emphasis on naming behaviors and reminding him to use self-calming strategies he had learned in therapy outside school. A behavior plan was highly successful for him in that he benefited from the visual feedback, consistent attention, and structure of the intervention. In addition, he had a strong relationship with his teacher and classroom paraprofessional (who was essentially there to assist him, though she had been identified as a classroom helper rather than an individual aide). In spite of such supports, there were occasional times in which Phil would seem to snap, and loud, verbally aggressive behavior ensued. When this scenario arose, a safety plan was implemented that had been created by the school's crisis team. Typically, his para could coax him to a quiet area that had been set up across the hall, and Phil would rage in there for a period of time before calming down. No one would attempt to speak with him during this period of time because it would only fuel his anger. Fortunately, Phil was not physically aggressive, which would have led to a discussion concerning the need for physical restraint or, more likely for a child this age, a different school placement. On rare occasions, Phil refused to leave the classroom. In this situation, the other children were taken to the library, and the paraprofessional and school counselor would stay with him until he regained control. What this example illustrates is that an array of interventions is needed to help children with complicated behavior.

As this chapter shows, an effective behavioral intervention must be fundamentally both structured and fluid. At the same time, it needs to account for developmental and other factors that affect the real world of children's lives. Changes to these interventions are an expected aspect, yet they must be introduced to children, openly discussed, and integrated into the feedback process. Without sustained attention to these latter components, the structure of the plan will likely be destroyed, and it will lose its effectiveness. Adults able to do so have greater success in implementing the model.

Chapter 6

CASE STUDIES

This chapter will apply the behavioral model and principles from previous chapters by describing and analyzing specific case presentations. These cases represent an amalgam of actual consulting cases I have had over the years and, as such, are not specific to any one child. I have chosen this technique to protect individuals' privacy.

Paul

Paul was in seventh grade when he was referred by his school for outside consultation. A fidgety, complicated, and very humorous 13-year-old boy with a partially French Canadian (and otherwise unknown) background, he was diagnosed with combined-type ADHD, oppositional defiant disorder, and multiple learning disabilities. His past was notable for its history of early foster care, substantiated charges of abuse and neglect, and a subsequent adoption that separated him from his birth brother. Paul reported that he had been placed on a number of behavior plans over the years, all of which had been punitively oriented. Stimulant medication was used in an attempt to reduce the core symptoms of his ADHD. He readily acknowledged his challenging behavior and could cite verbatim the school's rules, but it was his impulsivity and poor problem solving in group settings that led to many of his difficulties. Teachers disliked having him in their classes because he often ended up in the middle of disruptive exchanges with other students. Consequences, such as trips to the principal, detentions, and internal suspensions, had no impact on his behavior, even though he committed each time to trying to do better. Paul was genuinely remorseful when he caused difficulties for others—though not in the moment—which left me in doubt about his diagnosis of oppositional defiant disorder. His ADHD label, on the other hand, was indisputable.

Consultation focused both on establishing the behavior plan and altering his school environment. For the latter, the most significant change was allowing him regular time in the woodworking shop. Not surprisingly, the school had resisted such a move, deciding instead to make this time contingent on improved behavior. There was much discussion about Paul as a potential safety risk, even though there was no history of problems in this setting. In fact, the teacher noted that he had very few difficulties with Paul and that he seemed calm and focused when working in the woodshop. In light of such observations, I recommended that Paul spend a regularly scheduled period per day in shop, a time that could not be removed unless his behavior in that setting warranted it. The school, after much deliberation, agreed to this. Paul flourished in the class. He produced a number of detailed, beautiful pieces and revealed himself to be truly talented in this hands-on area. An additional recommendation was to allot a period of 15 minutes per day for Paul to receive help with organizing his work. Because he often got off to a poor start in his classes, his behavior would spiral downward from there. The organizational help allowed him to review teacher directions, understand the focus of his assignments, and develop timetables. Given this, Paul was less anxious and fidgety when he entered his classes, such that he was somewhat less prone to setting off other students with his comments. Finally, and to its vast credit, the school offered both Paul and other students a guided academics period rather than an unsupervised study. The study period had historically been "a nightmare," and for Paul, it magnified all of his difficulties in unstructured situations. The guided academics period became a time to review work, bolster the areas where he struggled academically, and even get some of his homework done. As a result, his performance in school improved considerably.

Because the behavior plan was implemented at the same time as the other interventions, there is no way, from a scientifically controlled perspective, to discern which interventions made the most difference. To my way of thinking, it was the confluence of events that might be understood as an ecological set of changes. The school offered a series of environmental modifications that made sense for Paul developmentally and psychologically, and Paul made interrelated strides in his self-control. Both were necessary. The behavioral intervention contributed to the latter. Paul was enthused by the plan, especially because it offered him the opportunity to earn rewards (time to draw, time on the computer) and because it meant he had regular and predictable times to interact with his teachers. I think Paul was urgently seeking feedback for his behavior, but owing to an almost profound level of ADHD symptoms, he could not consistently make sense of how he was doing or, in his terms, "where he was heading." The regular discussion of his behavior permitted him, perhaps for the first time, to develop strategies for identifying problematic situations and ways to avoid the habitual downward spiral. It also let him know, on a relational level, that he was seen and understood by adults, which allowed for new avenues of positive, rather than negative, attention. By no means was Paul suddenly an easy student to have in class, but no one denied his progress. He was more productive, confident, and generally better in control of his behavior.

Lawrence

Lawrence is an 11-year-old, Caribbean American sixth grader who told me directly that he calls himself black and identifies with the African American students in his school. Obviously bright, teachers raved about his intelligence amid their concerns for his behavior. Lawrence was given an early diagnosis of bipolar disorder, complicated by a paternal family history of the disorder. Various behavioral interventions had come and gone over the years, along with multiple medications. Often, he was viewed as out of control and slow to calm down and had spent much time outside of the regular classroom, with ongoing consideration of placing him in an out-of-district behavioral program. Yet, because he consistently had periods in which his behavior and performance would improve, at least temporarily, the school had been reluctant to push for an outside placement.

I proposed a behavioral intervention that, though no one would openly admit it, prompted extensive eye-rolling by teachers and administrators in the school. They had tried various models without success, but seemingly without any real sense of how to implement a formal plan from a teaching perspective. I suggested regular feedback, such that Lawrence met with a teacher or paraprofessional at the end of each period. Consistent with the discussion in chapter 4, I also recommended that he participate in the discussion of the plan, specifically in terms of setting goals and establishing reward options. None of these strategies had been attempted in any of the previous efforts to set up a plan, nor had any kind of consistent feedback been formalized as part of the process. Given the level of difficulty Lawrence had experienced in the time leading up to the introduction of the plan, I asked that rewards be provided three times per day to start. Additionally, I needed to convince both school staff and his parents that the rewards should be provided in school rather than at home.

Lawrence made slow but meaningful gains via this intervention. While he remained a child whose moods cycled and who was easily angered, there was, overall, a noticeable softening of affect and associated behavior. When I asked him about his sense of the plan two weeks after it had been initiated, he told me that he enjoyed the regular talk time with adults in the school. It provided him a connection with teachers that he had not experienced before since most of his interactions with them had been based on his getting into trouble. Having to confront negative stories about himself became less painful since he knew that he would also hear about the positive things he did. Because he was reflective in his psychological makeup, he articulated that he experienced the intervention as a sort of anchor, in that he could tell how he was doing by looking at the sheet and attempting to adjust accordingly. When he was angry or felt overwhelmed, spoken language was difficult for him to process, and it was the visual feedback from the sheet that enabled him to gain a sense of how he was performing. He was highly motivated by the available rewards, and it seemed that this was linked to his having shorter periods of rage—in his words, he was quicker to "get through the storm." Clearly a behavior plan is not a cure for bipolar disorder, but it improved Lawrence's general behavior, raised his level of trust, and allowed him a new way of understanding the feedback he was offered by adults. The relationship building that accompanied these predictable and increasingly positive interactions was an important foundation for his relative increase in self-control. An ancillary benefit was that his psychiatrist began to request copies of the daily sheets (rather than voluminous pages of narrative log entries) as a concrete way to gauge Lawrence's response to medication.

Notably, Lawrence was one of two children of color in his classroom. This was a consistent occurrence in his experience of school, and Lawrence eventually confided that he had always felt that racism was a significant component of his behavioral struggles. His parents, too, seemed to hold this idea. It was, apparently, a result of more affirming interactions from using the behavior plan that made him think his teachers did not "hate him." I am not denying the real presence of racism and other forms of discrimination that occur in schools, just as they arise elsewhere in our culture, but in this particular instance, regular communication with his teachers offered him a new framework for observing and understanding his challenges.

James

James, a white 11-year-old fifth grader, presented a complicated picture immediately on his arrival at an urban, mixed-ethnic elementary school. This was a school already reeling from the sudden death of one of its main administrators as well as other losses to the school community. Given this scenario, there was a distinct lack of adult resources when James bounded into school for his first day. In combination with his history and experience, it made for anything but an auspicious beginning.

James intermittently lived with his father but also had a track record of living in foster homes, a series of placements that never lasted for long before he would return to his familiar family. His mother disappeared soon after his birth, and as an only child, he experienced himself as close to his father, even though he had been removed from the home on multiple occasions. In the current climate, he was again in a new foster home and clearly displeased by it. Rages, threats, and work refusal did not land him where he wanted to be—with his father—who had been placed in a rehab facility to treat alcohol and drug dependency. James had a strong will and a singular focus on his goal, but these attributes—which are advantageous when applied in the right situation—were a problem in school. Children were frightened of him, and frankly, so were many of the teachers.

A behavioral intervention was introduced. The look on James's face when this was raised should have told us everything we needed to know, but the school nonetheless went forward. He refused to participate in any discussion of the plan and what he might want to earn. He practically spit on the sheet when it was initially shown to him. As an outside impression, it appeared that he reexperienced that he was being controlled by adults who, in his way of thinking, did not care about him. Since he had managed to "escape" (his term) a number of foster homes in the past, my guess was that he assumed he would do the same in this instance.

The behavior plan was problematic from the outset. Rather than having no effect, it seemed to make things worse. Many times, when James received a not-earn, he would escalate to the point in which he needed to be removed from the classroom. Sometimes he went willingly, but other times, he did not. His behavior was reportedly similar with his foster parents, and they made it clear that he could not continue living in their home. While James had been diagnosed somewhere along the way with PTSD and oppositional defiant disorder, to me he was the personification of those labels: he was miserable, scared, and extremely angry. While his teacher continued to try to reach out to him, there was little response to these overtures. Finally, a few weeks into his stay, James broke a window at his foster home and was placed in a residential setting for boys with serious behavioral issues. This is a sad story but not a unique one, and it demonstrates that a behavioral intervention will provide little in the way of real help unless other aspects of a child's life are stabilized. For James, the only way to calm things was to place him in a structured, therapeutic setting; that is, the environment needed to change to try to address his emotional and behavioral needs. The irony was not lost on school staff, who, while debriefing from the whole experience, noted that his father required a similar setting at the same time.

Lisa

Lisa is nine years old, white (of Irish and Italian descent), and in third grade. Diagnosed with generalized anxiety disorder and provisionally with panic attacks, Lisa missed a significant number of school days during both the first and second grades. Supportive individual psychotherapy, help to the family from a local mental health agency, and, subsequently, medication via her pediatrician (a selective serotonin reuptake inhibitor—first Paxil, then Prozac) had little impact on her functioning. She was allowed to leave class as needed and had ongoing access to the school counselor. Contrary to the school's expectations, a psychological assessment revealed nothing in the way of specific learning needs, known history of trauma, or medical concerns, though there was a documented maternal family history of mood disorders (mainly depression). Generally, she was viewed by staff as a sweet but anxious child.

My experience is that adults in general and schools in particular are reluctant to employ consequences for children who exhibit anxious behavior as the primary reason for underperformance. If, however, one views the behavior plan as a supportive measure rather than a form of punishment, it is easier to accept the rationale for using it. In this case, Lisa had resisted all previous attempts by mental health professionals to teach her specific anxiety-reducing techniques, implying that the anxiety was beyond her control and therefore not worth risking the necessary effort. Her parents, it appeared, held a similar view. Given this context, we discussed the behavior plan with Lisa, engaging her around the goals of maintaining herself in the classroom and the particular rewards she could earn. To be honest, everyone held their breath, as there was legitimate concern that such an intervention would frustrate and perhaps anger her. The outcome was the converse: she made rapid gains. The focus on attending classes (and earning concrete rewards for doing this) and participating in the larger world of the school allowed her to glimpse a different way of managing herself, such that she began to seek help with ways to reduce anxiety. Consistent with the research of Wilson (2002),[73] it was the experience of her getting through the anxiety that spurred further success. The behavioral intervention was a catalyst, though I believe Lisa was poised for success and just needed extrinsic help as a way to begin the process. Lisa relished reviewing the sheets with her teacher and school counselor and, with regular review meetings built into her daily schedule, discovered new ways to garner attention from the significant adults in her life. While she remained a somewhat worried, perfectionist third grader, her progress was tangible.

In Lisa's scenario, it was, therefore, her new and what might be considered courageous actions that opened up a different way for her to understand her anxiety, her relationships with others, and, ultimately, herself. Behavioral interventions, then, can contribute by generating fresh pathways that offer substantively more than simply modifying overtly negative behavior. Instead, they serve as a relationship-based vehicle for exploring and enacting healthy behaviors that stimulate further development and mastery.

Gregory

Gregory, a fourth grader from an intact and supportive family, is diagnosed with Tourette's syndrome, although he carried a number of other diagnoses before this was settled on. Initially, he was thought to have co-occurring ADHD and anxiety and then OCD as well. It was not until his parents convinced a pediatrician that he was also having tics (not due to medication and for longer than six months) that the new diagnosis was made. Gregory presented as defiant, in need of control, and hyperactive. He was also intelligent and aware of his struggles; as such, he held back his tics at school until earlier this school year when, under intense stress, he burst out with an assortment of facial and guttural tics. When I first observed him in the classroom, he was under a desk refusing to get up. This event was emblematic of the kinds of issues he and his school were confronted with almost every day.

Tourette's in children is often poorly understood. This is as true for medical providers as it is for schools. Tics are correlated with anxiety in that they increase with higher levels of stress. Certainly this seemed true for Gregory. The need for control is both a need to understand and predict the environment and a personality style that tends toward the idiosyncratic; that is, what is important to a child with Tourette's locked into completing a task is finishing, not moving on in a timely fashion as dictated by others. The inherent disparity between what the child and teacher each needs in the moment underlies a good deal of the behavioral issues that arise in schools.

Consultation, to start, emphasized a number of environmental modifications. After these were instituted—and a frustrated staff was able to see that some interventions could actually work—a behavioral intervention was established. In cases in which the staff are essentially feeling hopeless about a child, it makes little sense to begin with a behavior plan because, most often, the plan will simply reflect such hopelessness. The first step was to educate everyone involved with Gregory about Tourette's. He and his parents wanted his classmates to know about it, so a forum was held that described the nature of the disorder. His mother was instrumental in the process and served as the primary speaker to both students and staff. Gregory, like many children who prefer to avoid the scrutiny built into such situations, chose not to attend. My impression was that the other children were fine with the information and unfazed by it, but his teachers had a harder time. Understandably, they wanted to make sure that the modifications did not translate into allowing Gregory to do whatever he wanted. But they did see him in a new light, especially his need to complete tasks once they were undertaken and his tendency to pace the room. We built so-called tic times into his schedule, and these were greatly beneficial to him: he lurched and jumped and made noises as much as he wanted in a private, quiet room, which allowed him to return to class in a noticeably calmer fashion. Similar to the approach used to help children with AS, the school modified his recess and lunch so that these became quieter, more contained activities. He ate in a classroom with three additional students and had recess in the gym with that same crew, which brought him a degree of relief from the social overstimulation he reported. Other children clamored to join him because, at least initially, they liked the access to the gym during recess and, frankly, the relative peace of lunch outside the cafeteria. All these changes required some creativity and effort on the part of the school, but there was a real willingness to implement such modifications because the principal was firmly behind them, and the school recognized that there would be a similar need among future students.

Once these changes were established, a behavior plan was begun. It focused solely on one goal: following directions. This was discussed openly and clearly, with Gregory gaining a reasonable understanding of what was expected from him. If he was not allowed to complete a task in the moment—though, at times, teachers accommodated him around this—he was promised a time that same day to do so. This contained his anxiety enough that he was usually able to move on when needed. And he was highly motivated by the reward options, which consisted of tickets he could use to earn either short-term or longer-term rewards. Initially, he wanted (and needed) a twice-daily reward, but gradually, he was able to wean this to a less frequent event. Finally, his parents consented to a medical evaluation. To me, this seemed a response to the school's attempts to help Gregory, as they had perceived that any mention of the possibility of medication was simply an attempt to punish him and avoid making necessary changes. It was the pediatrician

who had done most of the advocacy for this, but it was when his
parents observed his emergent success but unabated high anxiety
that they went ahead with the evaluation. Gregory began a small
trial of Prozac, which, two weeks later, appeared to take the edge
off his anxiety amid a small reduction in his tics. This is a success
story but one that illustrates how the hard work of a child's team
can lead to a number of positive changes.

Fernando

Fernando is a first grader, almost seven years old, the middle of
three children, and very angry in terms of his posture and facial
expressions. Both his parents are from Puerto Rico, and although
they have been in Massachusetts for a number of years, they continue to converse mainly in Spanish. When Fernando was in his
first year of preschool, his father was seriously injured in an accident at work, leaving him partially paralyzed and unable to work.
There was a reported history of marital difficulties, and the parents
had previously separated, though Fernando's mother moved back
in with her husband after his accident. The department of social
services had been intermittently involved with the family.

Fernando was known in school for acting in a controlling manner
as well as for the severity of his outbursts, which seemed linked to
denying him what he wanted, but he was not predictable in this.
No formal learning issues were documented, though behavioral
concerns had been noted since preschool. These included poor
spatial boundaries and impulsivity, though he was not fidgety or
disorganized. Moodiness and poor frustration tolerance were also
observed, as were episodes of graphically violent play. In contrast to these distressing accounts, Fernando was reported to be
affectionate with adults, generally willing to help when asked, and
close to a number of his teachers. In spite of the fact that teachers
sometimes walked on eggshells around him, there was a strong
bond that seemed to be established.

A number of environmental modifications were attempted.
Primarily, Fernando was pulled back—in a physical sense—from
other children, especially during group activities, when he was
most likely to get angry. He was not separated from others, just
given a bit of extra room. The school counselor worked with him
on ways to maintain personal space, teaching him, for example, the

one-arm's-length rule. Although he was an enthusiastic participant in skills instruction, Fernando was silent and shut down about his life at home. Play therapy was provided for him within the school setting, but he did not actively or willingly participate. In spite of these interventions, Fernando remained angry and continued to have difficulty getting along with other children.

The behavioral intervention was instituted. While Fernando was excited by the prospect of earning rewards (the grab bag, special time with an adult, computer games), he could not maintain the success he initially demonstrated with the plan. He did very well the first three days, began to decline, and then, by the second week, returned to his earlier patterns of behavior. The data sheets illustrated what teachers had reported all along: that he was random in his behavior, and there was no particular pattern to his outbursts.

In this case, the behavior plan functioned more as an informational tool than a method of change. The arbitrariness of his behavior suggested that he was not responding solely to the immediate events in his environment. As it turned out, the school collaborated closely with the department of social services and, at one point, shared the results of its various attempts to help Fernando, including the outcome from using the behavior plan. With further investigation, it became evident that Fernando was a witness to ongoing domestic violence and had been physically victimized as well. While the subsequent story took on complicated twists and turns, the father was removed from the home, and over time, Fernando's rages diminished. When I saw him last, the angry look had been replaced by a more open, if not sad, countenance. An addendum to the case is that, many months later, the school again employed the behavioral intervention as a way to help Fernando with specific social behaviors. Given his change in circumstances, he made reasonable and steady progress.

A theme of these six cases is the importance of developing a hypothesis about children's behavior and responding with a combination of environmental, relational, and behavioral interventions. In this case, as in so many others, it was critical for school staff to try to understand the nature of the presenting problems and what it meant about the child. This is not a linear process, but one of trial and error, careful observation, and respect for children's real-life circumstances. Only in this way can we help them in their efforts to make sense of and challenge their own patterns of behavior.

Chapter 7

GOING FORWARD

This final chapter addresses different ideas for moving into the future with the aim of developing a more cohesive, thoughtful plan of action. Areas of practice research that deserve attention are noted, as are innovative approaches that show promise. Clearly, while the topic of behavioral health is an active one in schools and among community- and school-based clinicians, there remains much that we do not yet grasp about children's behavior and how to help them with this.

RESTITUTION (OR RESTORATIVE JUSTICE)

An approach to countering negative behavior, one that extends substantively beyond a simple not-earn on a behavioral intervention, is known as *restitution*. As noted earlier, behavioral interventions do not replace a school's discipline code or other policy responses to aggressive or antisocial behavior. While behavioral interventions appear to have varying levels of success, based on a host of relational, environmental, and intrinsic factors, I have argued that there are core attributes that contribute to a higher likelihood of success. Above all, they must be conducted in an atmosphere that promotes a positive outcome. Similarly, there must be a tone of respect and safety that infuses the larger school environment.

One way to translate such lofty ideas into actual practice is to explore the ways schools successfully ensure safety and teach respectful behavior.

A particularly useful approach is restitution, sometimes referred to as reparative or restorative justice. The general notion is that, as a result of some type of social infraction, a child should concretely make amends directly to the other child, rather than solely to school authorities via detention or suspension. In the same vein, a child who vandalizes property would need to make it up to the community as a whole instead of a single authority figure. The Center for Restorative Justice, at Suffolk University in Massachusetts, operationalizes restorative justice on its Web site as a matter of *values* (with respect identified as the predominant one), *process* (for "victims, wrongdoers, and communities"), and specified *practices*. These practices, while defined and implemented in varying ways among the different constituencies that utilize this approach, essentially focus on ways to give back to others when this is needed. Generally, restitution is viewed as both a legal and ethical methodology, but I see it as equally a behavioral one due to its emphasis on teaching skills and encouraging better choices.

A short example follows: Brianna bullied another girl, Miranda, in her sixth-grade classroom by making up stories about things she had allegedly said about other girls. The result was a tearful child who did not want to come to school and felt ostracized by the other girls. When the teacher discovered what had happened, she had Brianna write a note for the girls in her class explaining her behavior. In addition, the teacher gave Brianna the task of carrying Miranda's lunch tray for one week, such that she missed out on valued social time. As the victim, Miranda felt supported in this scenario, and Brianna appeared to have learned a useful lesson. As it turns out, this was not the first time Brianna had engaged in such behavior. She usually "got into trouble" with a teacher or school administrator, but things generally—in her terms—"blew over," and after a little while, she would renew her pattern of bullying other girls she felt threatened by. The regular consequences were ineffective at altering her behavior, and until restitution was employed, she seemed to have learned very little about how to change her behavior or take responsibility for it.

Juvenile court systems have adopted similar approaches in the effort to teach first-time offenders more adaptive, socially responsible behavior and divert them from restrictive placements. In my experience, restitution tends to be used on a consistent basis only by specific court systems and within substantially separate (or other alternative) classroom programs. But all schools would benefit from employing such interventions in an ongoing way. Restitution can serve important preventive and teaching functions with any child and can be incorporated into the regular practice of any school or classroom. One school district in Minnesota, for example (Stinchcomb, Bazemore, & Riestenberg, 2006), found that by integrating restorative justice principles into its middle and high schools, there was a decrease in the number of suspensions, expulsions, and "behavioral referrals."[74] More research into this topic is clearly needed.

While I have simplified the model to an extent, it is worth noting as a valuable complement to the types of approaches I have advocated throughout this book. A distinct benefit is that it goes beyond traditional thinking about punishment in that children are required to come face-to-face with the people and larger communities affected by their behavior. In this, it offers compelling opportunities for learning and has the potential as well to bring greater solace to those who have been harmed.

THE STAGES OF CHANGE MODEL

Another way of conceptualizing behavior is to understand that the motivation for change is variable and occurs along a spectrum. A specific example is the Stages of Change model depicted by Prochaska, Norcross, and DiClemente (1994).[75] In essence, these researchers, who are credited with developing a transtheoretical model (one that could apply to any therapeutic theory or approach), address the therapeutic question of an individual's readiness for change. They suggested a continuum of preparedness, starting with what they refer to as precontemplation and moving through contemplation, preparation, action, and maintenance. What these stages imply is the distinction between the belief, on one end, that one does not have a problem at all and, at the other, that there is a problem requiring continued monitoring and the effort to maintain effective helping strategies. Consistent with any stage-oriented model, the inherent weakness is that it can appear as though people move in a linear direction, rather than in a more circular or back-and-forth fashion. Progress is rarely a straight line to the top. The researchers are careful to note this, but it remains a tantalizing (and wishful) idea that people could be predictable to such a degree. In spite of this, their model opens up new ways of thinking about therapeutic work and addressing the notion of resistance.

Similar to other areas discussed in this book, there is limited evidence that such thinking has been applied to real-life behavioral approaches. Prochaska et al.'s (1994) model has been employed in work with adults, including those with substance abuse issues, but apparently not in the context of interventions with children.[76] In spite of their consistent usage in schools and other settings, behavioral interventions have suffered from their lack of connection to cutting-edge theory development. One might, for example, refine the goal setting and feedback processes of the intervention based on where one perceives a child is located along the spectrum of readiness. For instance, a child who tends to blame others and rarely if ever accepts responsibility could be rewarded simply for acknowledging his role in a problematic situation, rather than setting the bar higher and expecting him to solve the problem.

Similarly, one might attempt to engage a family based on this assessment. For example, a family in the contemplation stage that is beginning to recognize—and accept—that a child's behavior is problematic can be asked what it might take to get them to take action around this such as setting stronger limits, seeing a pediatrician, or seeking outside therapy. The questions we ask should be determined by our sensitivity to the family's readiness to intervene. We also need to discern the family's willingness to accept that the child might need a behavioral intervention while in school, or the plan—in some instances—could be disparaged if not sabotaged at home. The point here is that the effectiveness of behavioral interventions would be enhanced by grounding their usage in a more expansive understanding of children and their life circumstances.

SOCIAL SKILLS TRAINING

As discussed earlier in the book, there is increasing attention to the idea that social skills can be taught, especially in children who lack the intuitive capacity to interact successfully with their peers. Some existing models for teaching these skills address whole classrooms, based on the assumption that all children can benefit from combining their academic and social learning. Two such models are Responsive Classroom and Second Step. While a number of schools and teachers are familiar with one or both, many are not. In short—and in different ways—these approaches emphasize the social and emotional aspects of child development, based on a belief that the idea of curriculum should be broader and more inclusive than only the focus on academics. While this seems to fly in the face of the current federal mandate to increase schools' emphasis on academic learning, both these programs emphasize practical and focused strategies for achieving their goals. In reality, they can save time based on the problems they prevent, and concurrently, they aim to leave children more prepared and accessible for learning. While the evidence is being gathered in support of these types of programs, they offer a promising direction for augmenting our approaches to helping children.

AREAS FOR FURTHER STUDY

As mentioned, a significant finding reported in *Education Week* was that informative research concerning student discipline has not been successfully integrated into the practice approaches of schools (Viadero, 2002).[77] Given such a finding, it is critical that we persist in seeking out ways to disseminate and incorporate *best practices* into the culture of our school communities. Such efforts have been made on behalf of psychotherapy (see Hubble, Duncan, & Miller, 1999), and much could be gleaned from this body of work to direct the search for improving our school-centered practices.[78] Otherwise, an amalgam of approaches will continue to descend on teachers and school counselors, with no clear sense as to what works. Over the years, numerous teachers have reported that they feel confused by how they are supposed to respond to challenging students—it is a primary reason that teachers leave the profession. Many highly experienced teachers indicate that they survive by developing their own techniques based on what, on an individual basis, seemed effective for them. We need to do better in this.

I should note that "what works" is a contextual statement in that all of us who interact regularly with children need more information as to what is effective for whom, when, and in what circumstances. In the real world of children, nothing is successful in every situation, and claims to the contrary are simply false—children are not predictable in how they respond to adult direction or help. This complexity is what should drive us to conduct further exploration. Ideally, such research would join practitioners with professional investigators so that we study what we actually need to know. Teachers, counselors, parents—and children themselves—are best suited to determine the questions to ask. In addition, it is a mission of social justice for some investigators who study and address childhood poverty. We need to extrapolate from their findings the factors we should address empirically.

For example, additional qualitative and quantitative studies of children's relationships with adults in schools would help to identify and clarify the salience of these and shed light on particular factors children experience as valuable. Surprisingly little is known about such factors. Research that illuminates this information would be a strong starting point for developing supplementary and innovative helping strategies.

While no apparent research exists concerning the prevalence of behavioral interventions in schools or the gender breakdown of children placed on individual plans, it seems clear that boys are the primary recipients. In my experience, girls receive these less than one-tenth as often. Perhaps such a finding can be construed as roughly consistent with the clinic-referred prevalence rates of particular diagnoses such as ADHD (the impulsive/hyperactive and combined types) and the range of identified behavioral disorders (oppositional defiant disorder, conduct disorder). Nonetheless, future research should more fully investigate prevalence rates and demographic factors such as the child's diagnostic category, gender, socioeconomic status, race, and ethnicity. More detailed and systematic information concerning who receives formal behavioral interventions would allow researchers to qualitatively study the meaning of such support for different subgroups of children. Furthermore, it will help in our understanding of why particular children are assigned this form of help and others are not.

Similarly, developing a larger set of data as to whether behavioral interventions are successful (and in what ways, for whom, etc.) would considerably enrich our current knowledge base. There may be a presumption of efficacy that is simply not warranted by careful analysis. This is especially important since school-based behavioral interventions appear to be so much a common response to challenging behavior. Clearly we need further information to refine our approaches. Moreover, a deeper understanding of whether particular schools or school districts have greater success in employing behavioral strategies should shed light on how those schools implement such interventions—and what else they offer children that contributes to their developmental and behavioral growth.

Given the widespread challenges we share communally in helping children, we should do everything possible to learn more about children's behavior, enhance our methods for reaching out to them, and refine our approaches to intervention. All of us—teachers, parents, clinicians, researchers, and administrators, along with the children we serve—must participate purposefully in this vital endeavor. Since the introduction to this book began with a question about meaning, the ending will do the same: what could have more meaning for our future than this?

BIBLIOGRAPHY

INTRODUCTION

1. Miller, W. R., & Rollnick, S. (2002). *Motivational interviewing: Preparing people for change*. New York: Guilford Press.
2. Saari, C. (1992). The person-in-environment reconsidered: New theoretical bridges. *Child and Adolescent Social Work Journal, 9*, 205–219.

CHAPTER 1

3. Saphier, J., & Gower, R. (1997). *The skillful teacher*. Acton, MA: Research for Better Teaching.
4. Glicken, M. D. (2003). *Using the strengths approach in social work practice: A positive approach for the helping professions*. Boston: Allyn & Bacon/Longman.
5. Saleebey, D. (1996). The strengths perspective in social work practice: Extensions and cautions. *Social Work, 41*, 296–305.
6. McNeil, C. B. (1996). Aversive-nonaversive issue: Tip of the iceberg. *Child and Family Behavior Therapy, 18*, 17–28.
7. Eisenberger, R., & Cameron, J. (1996). Detrimental effects of reward. *American Psychologist, 51*, 1153–1166.
8. Kohn, A. (1993). *Punished by rewards*. Boston: Houghton Mifflin.
9. Wachtel, P. (1977). *Psychoanalysis and behavior therapy*. New York: Basic Books.

10. Goldstein, S. (1995). *Understanding and managing children's classroom behavior.* New York: John Wiley.

11. Thyer, B. A. (1988). Radical behaviorism and clinical social work. In R. A. Dorfman (Ed.), *Paradigms of clinical social work* (pp. 123–148). New York: Bruner/Mazel.

12. Viadero, D. (2002). Research on discipline not reaching schools. *Education Week, 22,* 10.

13. Brown, J., Dreis, S., & Nace, D. K. (1999). What really makes a difference in psychotherapy outcome? In M. Hubble, B. Duncan, & S. Miller (Eds.), *The heart and soul of change: What works in therapy* (pp. 389–447). Washington, DC: American Psychological Association.

14. Neimeier, G. J. (1995). The challenge of change. In R. A. Neimeyer & M. J. Mahoney (Eds.), *Constructivism in psychotherapy* (pp. 111–126). Washington, DC: American Psychological Association.

15. Olympia, D., & Larsen, J. (2005). Functional behavioral assessment: An emerging component of best school practices for ADHD. *ADHD Report, 13,* 1–5.

16. Crone, D. A., & Horner, R. H. (2003). *Building positive behavior support systems in schools.* New York: Guilford Press.

17. Ibid.

18. Ibid.

19. Friedberg, R. D., & McClure, J. M. (2002). *Clinical practice of cognitive therapy with children and adolescents.* New York: Guilford Press.

20. Drisko, J. W. (1999). Clinical work with mistrusting, aggressive, latency-age children. In N. Heller & T. Northcut (Eds.), *Enhancing psychodynamic therapy with cognitive-behavioral techniques* (pp. 157–181). Northvale, NJ: Jason Aronson.

21. Meichenbaum, D. (2003). *Treatment of individuals with anger control problems and aggressive behaviors.* Bethel, CT: Crown House.

22. Hubble, M. L., Duncan, B. L., & Miller, S. D. (1999). *The heart and soul of change: What works in therapy.* Washington, DC: American Psychological Association.

23. Marzano, R. J. (2003). *Classroom management that works: Research-based strategies for every teacher.* Alexandria, VA: Association for Supervision and Curriculum Development.

24. Poulsen, J. (2001). Facilitating academic achievement through affect attunement in the classroom. *Journal of Educational Research, 94,* 185–190.

25. Siegel, D. J., & Hartzell, M. (2003). *Parenting from the inside out: How a deeper self-understanding can help you raise children who thrive.* New York: Tarcher/Putnam.

26. Ibid.

27. Ibid.

28. Fraser, M. W. (1997). *Risk and resilience in childhood: An ecological perspective.* Washington, DC: NASW Press.

29. Robb, C. (2006). *This changes everything: The relational revolution in psychology.* New York: Farrar, Straus, and Giroux.

30. Cole, S. F., O'Brien, J. G., Gadd, M. G., Ristuccia, J., Wallace, D. L., & Gregory, M. (2005). *Helping traumatized children learn: Supportive school environments for children traumatized by family violence.* Boston, MA: Massachusetts Advocates for Children.

31. Dryfoos, J. G. (1994). *Full-service schools.* San Francisco: Jossey-Bass.

32. Rappaport, N., Flaherty, L. T., & Hauser, S. T. (2006). Beyond psycho-pathology: Assessing seriously disruptive students in school settings. *Journal of Pediatrics, 149,* 252–257.

CHAPTER 2

33. American Psychiatric Association. (2000). *Diagnostic and statistical manual of mental disorders* (4th ed., text rev.). Washington, DC: Author.

34. Tanguay, P. B. (2002). *Nonverbal learning disabilities at school: Educating students with NLD, Asperger syndrome, and related conditions.* Philadelphia: Jessica Kingsley. Tanguay also has a version for parents to assist them at home.

35. Thompson, S. (1997). *The source for nonverbal learning disorders.* East Moline, IL: LinguiSystems.

36. Attwood, Tony. (1998). *Asperger's syndrome: A guide for parents and professionals.* Philadelphia: Jessica Kingsley.

37. Chansky, T. E. (2004). *Freeing your child from anxiety.* New York: Broadway Books.

38. Foxman, P. (2004). *The worried child: Recognizing anxiety in children and helping them heal.* Alameda, CA: Hunter House.

39. Foa, E. B., & Wilson, R. R. (2001). *Stop obsessing: How to overcome your obsessions and compulsions.* New York: Bantam Books.

40. Kendall, P. (1992). *Coping cat workbook.* Ardmore, PA: Workbook.

41. Burns, D. D. (2006). *When panic attacks.* New York: Morgan Road Books.

42. Levine, J. E. (1997). "Factors associated with the assessment of attention deficit hyperactivity disorder (ADHD) among boys." *Dissertations Abstracts International, 59,* UMI 9820260.

43. Barkley, R. (2005). *ADHD and the nature of self-control.* New York: Guilford Press.

44. Greenwald, R. (2005). *Child trauma handbook: A guide for helping trauma-exposed children and adolescents.* New York: Haworth Press.

45. Silva, R. R. (2004). *Posttraumatic stress disorders in children and ado-lescents: Handbook.* New York: W. W. Norton.

46. Merrell, K. W. (2001). *Helping students overcome depression and anxiety: A practical guide.* New York: Guilford Press.

47. Goldstein, S., & Ingersoll, B. D. (2001). *Lonely, sad, and angry: How to help your unhappy child*. Plantation, FL: Specialty Press.

48. Greene, R. W. (2001). *The explosive child: A new approach for understanding and parenting easily frustrated, chronically inflexible children*. New York: HarperCollins.

49. Greene, R. W., & Ablon, J. S. (2006). *Treating explosive kids: The collaborative problem-solving approach*. New York: Guilford Press.

50. Bloomquist, M. L., & Schnell, S. V. (2002). *Helping children with aggression and conduct problems: Best practices for intervention*. New York: Guilford Press.

CHAPTER 3

51. Greene, R. W. (2001). *The explosive child: A new approach for understanding and parenting easily frustrated, chronically inflexible children*. New York: HarperCollins.

52. Hodgdon, L. A. (1995). *Visual strategies for improving communication: Practical supports for school and home*. Troy, MI: QuirkRoberts.

53. Gray, C. (2000). *The new social story book*. Arlington, TX: Future Horizons.

54. Goleman, D. (1995). *Emotional intelligence*. New York: Bantam Books.

55. Salovey, P., & Grewal, D. (2005). The science of emotional intelligence. *Current Directions in Psychological Science, 14*, 281–285.

56. McGinnis, E., Goldstein, A. P., Sprafkin, R. P., & Gershaw, N. J. (1984). *Skillstreaming the elementary school child: A guide for teaching prosocial skills*. Champaign, IL: Research Press.

57. McAfee, J. L. (2002). *Navigating the social world: A curriculum for individuals with Asperger's syndrome, high functioning autism, and related disorders*. Arlington, TX: Future Horizons.

58. Saphier, J., & Gower, R. (1997). *The skillful teacher*. Acton, MA: Research for Better Teaching.

59. Garbarino, J. (1995). *Raising children in a socially toxic environment*. San Francisco: Jossey-Bass.

60. Kozol, J. (2005). *The shame of the nation: The restoration of apartheid schooling in America*. New York: Crown.

61. Kozol, J. (1991). *Savage inequalities: Children in America's schools*. New York: Crown.

62. Kozol, J. (1995). *Amazing grace: The lives of children and the conscience of a nation*. New York: Crown.

63. Beck, A. T. (1999). *Prisoners of hate: The cognitive basis of anger, hostility, and violence*. New York: HarperCollins. Along with more than 500 publications, Beck also developed the Beck Hopelessness Scale in 1974, a 20-item measurement scale that is widely used to assess an individual's risk for suicide. See Beck, A. T., Weissman, A., Lester, D., & Trexler, L. (1974). The

measurement of pessimism: The Hopelessness Scale. *Journal of Consulting and Clinical Psychology, 42*, 861–865.

CHAPTER 4

64. Canter, L., & Canter, M. (1992). *Assertive discipline.* Santa Monica, CA: Lee Canter. A third edition was published in 2001 by the National Education Service.

65. Saleebey, D. (1996). The strengths perspective in social work practice: Extensions and cautions. *Social Work, 41*, 296–305.

66. Hill, R. D., Olympia, D., & Angelbuer, K. C. (1991). A comparison of preference for familial, social and material rewards between hyperactive and non-hyperactive boys. *School Psychology International, 12*, 225–229.

67. Hallowell, E. M., & Ratey, J. J. (1994). *Driven to distraction.* New York: Touchstone.

68. Applegate, J. S. (1997). The holding environment: An organizing metaphor for social work theory and practice. *Smith College Studies in Social Work, 68*, 7–29.

69. Cooley, M. L. (1998). Attention deficit disorder is an explanation, not an excuse. *ADHD Report, 6*, 13–14.

70. McGinnis, E., Goldstein, A. P., Sprafkin, R. P., & Gershaw, N. J. (1984). *Skillstreaming the elementary school child: A guide for teaching prosocial skills.* Champaign, IL: Research Press.

71. Schamess, G. (1996). Who profits and who benefits from managed mental health care? *Smith College Studies in Social Work, 66*, 209–220.

CHAPTER 5

72. Miller, W. R., & Rollnick, S. (2002). *Motivational interviewing: Preparing people for change.* New York: Guilford Press.

CHAPTER 6

73. Wilson, R. R. (2002). *Don't panic: Taking control of anxiety attacks.* New York: Harper-Perennial.

CHAPTER 7

74. Stinchcomb, J. B., Bazemore, G., & Riestenberg, N. (2006). Beyond zero tolerance: Restoring justice in secondary schools. *Youth Violence and Juvenile Justice, 4*, 123–147.

75. Prochaska, J. O., Norcross, J. C., & DiClemente, C. C. (1994). *Changing for good.* New York: William Morrow.

76. Ibid.

77. Viadero, D. (2002). Research on discipline not reaching schools. *Education Week, 22*, 10.

78. Hubble, M. A., Duncan, B. L., & Miller, S. D. (1999). *The heart and soul of change: What works in therapy.* Washington, DC: American Psychological Association.

INDEX

ABOUT THE AUTHOR

JAMES LEVINE, PhD, LICSW, is the founder and director of James Levine & Associates, P.C., a multidisciplinary consulting and psychotherapy company, with two sites in Massachusetts, that specializes in helping people of all ages with developmental, psychological, and behavioral difficulties. In addition to his own clinical practice, he has consulted to numerous schools and mental health agencies along with holding adjunct teaching posts in the graduate programs of the Simmons College and Smith College schools of social work. Dr. Levine lives in western Massachusetts with his wife and two children.